Splendid Hotels of Europe

First published in the United States by Turner Publishing, Inc.
Simultaneously published in France by Gallimard, and in Japan by Dohosha Publishing Co., Ltd.

Library of Congress Cataloging-in-Publication Data
Archimbaud, Nicholas d'.
[Portraits d'hôtels. English]
Splendid hotels of Europe: a photographic portrait/photographs by Nicholas d'Archimaud;
text by Bruno de Cessole, Séverine Jouve, Thierry Wolton; translated by Donnali Fifield. —1st ed.
p.   cm.
ISBN 1-57036-111-8
1. Hotels—Europe—Guidebooks—Pictorial works.   2. Europe—Guidebooks—Pictorial works.
I. De Cessole, Bruno.   II. Jouve, Séverine.   III. Wolton, Thierry.   IV. Title.
TX907.5.E85A7313   1994
647.94401—dc20   94-21043
                                                     CIP

Turner Publishing, Inc.
A Subsidiary of Turner Broadcasting System, Inc.
1050 Techwood Drive, N.W.
Atlanta, Georgia 30318

Distributed by Andrews and McMeel
A Universal Press Syndicate Company
4900 Main Street
Kansas City, Missouri 64112

First edition 10 9 8 7 6 5 4 3 2 1

Printed in Singapore

SPLENDID HOTELS of EUROPE

A PHOTOGRAPHIC PORTRAIT

Photographs by

Nicholas d'Archimbaud

Text by Bruno de Cessole, Séverine Jouve, Thierry Wolton
Translated by Donnali Fifield

Turner Publishing, Inc.

ATLANTA

CONTENTS

THE HOTEL OF MY MOST BEAUTIFUL MEMORIES

Valery Larbaud was a spiritual seeker; lover of art, books, travel, and women; and cosmopolitan par excellence, whose Muse was the daughter of world capitals. He knew and frequented the most sumptuous palace hotels as well as the simplest inns of Europe. This experience, if we are to believe him, did not leave only blissful memories: "I know," he wrote in *Yellow, Blue, White*, "that a hotel room has an almost unlimited power to isolate. A banal space, open to all comers, and which resembles time that will never pass quickly enough . . ." He wrote this, too, edged with bitterness: "Life in a hotel is a life half-lived, without character, the same under every climate, in every country, a type of school life, which it was good, perhaps, to have gone through, but which, if we return to it later, seems quite poor, futile, superficial. . . . It offers us always the same types in the same situations." Yet Larbaud also confessed that his sweetest reminiscences remained tied to the long stay he made, as a child, at the Grand Hôtel du Louvre: "Oh, I loved that hotel at the center of the world, more than the house where I was born, more than any of the housed where I spent my childhood. . . ."

Which Larbaud should we trust? The disillusioned one—embittered by illness that had so often confined him to a room, whether it be in a sanatorium, hospital, or hotel—or the nostalgic Larbaud, recalling, years later, "the hotel of my most beautiful memories" and its long corridors with their carpets of an unequaled softness, which had muffled his footsteps as a child? I am inclined to think that the voluptuous and melancholic author of the *Journal of A. O. Barnabooth* was more moved by the charms of hotel life than by its nuisances, even if he sometimes used the formula of Gaétan de Putouarey, one of his characters: "the large baggages in the best room of the best hotel, where we go only to fetch our letters, and the suitcase in a furnished room in an inn, where we live." Besides, where did Larbaud write most of his stories and essays if not in the propitious atmosphere of a salon or room in a luxury hotel.

To judge by the number of artists and writers who have used hotels to begin, pursue, or complete a work, there must be a mysterious link between creation and the work-cell offered by the "abstract" space of a hotel. Contrary to appearances, it is not in the calm and familiar intimacy of home that the spirit or the Muses take flight. Perhaps it is precisely a decor that disorients, a setting neutral enough not to fetter the imagination or attract attention, which artists require. In this respect, a hotel offers the incomparable advantage of being an ideal haven, the intermediate between the reclusive atmosphere of home and the noisy, impersonal, more or less hostile climate of public places.

Books, wrote Marcel Proust, are the children of solitude and silence. When he left his cork-lined room, which was transformed by the vapors of incense into the fantastic lair of some modern Pythia, the author of *Remembrance of Things Past* had his customary haunts at the Ritz, which for him was a second home. There he found the quality of silence and solitude necessary for his work. The staff knew him, and they respected the strange habits of this bone-chilled brother of Scheherazade, always wrapped up in coats and scarves, even in the height of summer. Whether fearing drafts, unknown faces, or the importunately curious, Proust preferred to receive and dine, several times a week, in his room at the Ritz.

When younger and in better health, he had made frequent stays at hotels in order to work—we know that he withdrew to a hotel in Fontainebleu to begin *Jean Santeuil*—or to spend the summer, as at the Hôtel des Roches Noires in Trouville and at the Grand Hôtel de Carbourg, which served as models for the Grand Hôtel de Balbec in *Within a Budding Grove*. And no one has analyzed better than Proust the sequence of contradictory impressions, the alternating apprehension and joy, that travelers feel alighting in an unknown hotel: from the anxious uneasiness felt discovering a room for the first time, and the many things which we do not know, up to the moment when, the unknown tamed, we settle into the familiarity of habits and pleasures, all the more delightful because we know them to be fleeting.

When age began to weigh down on him, it was in a palace hotel of old-world Europe that the sometimes moody, always changeable Vladimir Nabokov decided to take lodgings for the remainder of his days. In the old-fashioned wing of Montreux Palace, a huge beehive of four hundred rooms above Lake Leman, the author of *Lolita* was realizing the wish he had expressed as a penniless refugee in the Paris of the 1930s. To the question: "What is your dearest wish?" the exile had answered: "To be able to live in a grand hôtel de luxe." Tempted to buy a villa after a stay of several years at Montreux Palace, Nabokov finally chose to remain at the hotel, where he could lead an almost colonial style of life. Like Proust at the Ritz, he benefited from the discreet protection of the staff, who saw to it that he would not be bothered by autograph hunters or by overly curious tourists. And they obligingly satisfied his slightest desires, which were less eccentric, however, than Proust's. The latter was known to have ice-cold beer or a strawberry sorbet delivered to him at four in the morning. . . .

The golden rule of prestige hotels: strive to satisfy the hard to please, if not extravagant, desires and manias of their guests. This surely remains one of the attractions of hotel life, with the best hotels offering one the impression of not being an ordinary guest, anonymous and interchangeable, but someone they are glad to welcome, pamper, and see return. Such is the spirit of most of the hotels whose flagrant beauties and secret charms this book reveals. In this respect, Valery Larbaud's unkind comment about the "life without character" led at a hotel is stripped of pertinence, so much do these hotels cultivate their differences and show themselves able to respond to the most diverse wishes.

There are some hotels where we would like to live for the space of a few days—a heartrending passion such as that known by Louis Aragon and Nancy Cunard at Hôtel de Giverny.

Others could lend themselves to the ceremony of goodbyes at the end of a love affair, such as the Daniell was for George Sand and Alfred de Musset, in Venice.

Some are lively enough to want to open a boutique of wit, as Lady Emerald Cunard, once upon a time, held a salon at the Dorchester in London and at the Ritz Carlton in New York.

Some are so restful that we would like to be extremely tired in order to have the privilege of relaxing in them.

Others are so hospitable that we want to set down our bags there for the rest of our days, as Coco Chanel did at the Ritz.

And why not end one's life there, above one's means, like Oscar Wilde, the impecunious and fallen tenant of Hôtel d'Alsace, on the rue des Beaux-Arts in Paris? When he died, forgotten by all and held in contempt by philistines, just a handful of his old friends followed his coffin. Among them, only one was generous enough to offer a wreath to the former prince of dandies. It was the owner—still unpaid—of Hôtel d'Alsace. On the wreath read this sober dedication: "To my lodger . . ."

CHÂTEAU DE BAGNOLS

~

"Je laisse ma famille, une famille désolée,
et je pars pour Bagnols."

Mme de Sévigné

Arabesque Victorian-style lawn chairs on the esplanade, shaded by linden trees. Guests dine here in summer (left).

View from the loggia, opening onto the terrace and its bay of lavender (below, left).

Under a vault speckled with an ornamental feather pattern, the space in the Hunt Room—decorated in the manner of Antonio Tempesta—is treated like a vast underbrush, through which hunters advance (below, right).

When you arrive at Château de Bagnols, as the warm morning light caresses the velvet-softness of its renowned "golden stones," you experience the extraordinary sensation of having reached one of the high places of art. With its towers, its moats, and its access through a drawbridge, Bagnols reveals itself to be a historical landmark of the first rank, which presupposes a meticulous restoration of each of its parts. Adding to that is the magic of its surroundings, so distinctive to the Beaujolais region, in the heart of which the château stands out like a masterpiece.

We owe the château's renaissance to its current owners, Helen and Paul Hamlyn, who acquired it in 1987. Indeed, Lord and Lady Hamlyn, brilliantly assisted by their architect Tom Wilson and by Jean-Gabriel Mortamet, the inspector general for historical monuments, took care not to diminish its historical character. The remarkable human resources, technical and financial, that were put into service

Photos on pages 10, 11, 12 and 13:

Page 10: *The richly worked mirror in the living room of the Madame de Sévigné Suite reflects eighteenth-century panels, painted on the theme of imaginary castles. The panels' mellow colors agree with the subdued tones of the Directoire armchairs.*

Page 11: *On the east façade, the morning light plays on the "golden stones" of the ancient thirteenth-century donjon. The shadows are cast by trees on the large terrace* (top).
A corner of the orchard reconverted into a French-style garden: squares of box trees bordered by yews, mythological statues, and a cool alley interrupted by the basin of a fountain (bottom, left).
The exuberance of wisteria softens the rigorous beauty of this paneled fifteenth-century door leading into an interior court (bottom, right).

Pages 12 and 13: *From the bottom of the garden, Ariadne and Bacchus, sculpted in 1763, contemplate the utterly medieval severity of the château's south façade whose central porch opens onto the Guards' Hall.*

In the drawing room of the Geoffroy de Balzac Suite, the warm atmosphere created by the vault's ochers attenuates the thickness of the walls. On the mantel of the Gothic fireplace, the coat of arms of the lords of Balzac.

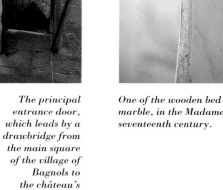

The principal entrance door, which leads by a drawbridge from the main square of the village of Bagnols to the château's reception hall.

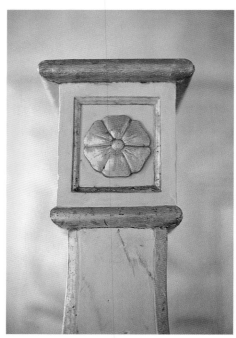

One of the wooden bed posters, painted to imitate marble, in the Madame de Sévigné Suite. Pure seventeenth century.

Detail from the astonishing trompe l'oeil decor of the Grand Salon, enhancing eighteen tableaux, a number of them false pediments and pilasters.

during the château's four years of restoration proves it to us at every step.

The beginning of its existence dates back to the year 1217. During the age of chivalry, Château de Bagnols was the property of the lords d'Oingt, allied with the archbishop of Lyons. Thanks to his patronage, Guichard d'Oingt was able to acquire nearby Château de Chatillon, and undertook the construction of Bagnols, which lasted until 1221. On his death, his son Etienne inherited de Baignous (Bagnols) and made a favorable marriage with Artaude de Roussillon. The estates were entrusted to her cousin, Artaud V de Roussillon-Annonay.

Today, only three round towers and a few interior walls remain of the original pentagonal design. Built into rock, equipped with curved walls that connected circular towers topped by battlements, Bagnols was a veritable bastion jutting out over the valley.

During the reign of Charles VIII, the château fulfilled several functions: as the temporary residence for the lord, the administrative center for the area, and as the fortress during times of war. Three main buildings from this period are still identifiable: the Guards' Hall and the two non-aligned buildings that face it.

Jeanne, the only daughter of Antoine d'Albon, married Roffec de Balzac in 1453 and brought as her dowry the lordships of Châtillon and Bagnols. Roffec had the north tower built; its horseshoe structure later proved ideal for defense. Bagnols then passed to the second of his sons, Geoffroy, lord of Montrillon and chamberlain to the king. (Charles VIII would visit the château the following year, 1490.)

At the beginning of the sixteenth

Glimpse of the château's sports activities. The "very rich hours" of gentlemen of leisure in the twenties.

Before going to dinner in the Guards' Hall, a cocktail on the large terrace of the château, which dominates the hill over the Lyons region.

In the Grand Salon, the Renaissance fireplace in white stone inlaid with deep blue marble, a sculptured jewel set off by the sofas' rosy fabric.

century, the fortress' austerity was toned down: the enceinte was capped with round turrets and the interior court's four façades were perforated for mullion windows. The Guards' Hall was enriched by a monumental chimney decorated with carved figures, whose central part—the escutcheon of France—is still preserved today.

In 1566, the lordship of Bagnols became the property of Jehan Camus. He died in 1568, leaving the estate to his son Claude. The latter undertook renovation work on the joists before having the framework for the west wing built. Different types of loop-holes seen on the chateau's west façade, as well as a portal equipped with a defense system unique in the region, date from the time of the religious wars. Claude's son Charles sold the property to Gaspard Dugué in 1619. Dugué, the treasurer of France, in his turn undertook considerable repairs, which did not end until 1639.

Converting the feudal château into a country seat, Gaspard Dugué set up outbuildings, created a parterre garden, did away with the drawbridge, erected an embossed portal with a triangular pediment at the entrance, furnished the large drawing room on the first floor with a monumental fireplace, and decorated the rooms with wall paintings unique for the richness of their drawings, which were inspired by motifs on silk from the school of Lyons. It was in such a decor that his grandson Dreux Louis received his cousin, Madame de Coulanges, and in 1672, the celebrated letter-writer Madame de Sévigné.

In 1711, the château was sold to Barthélémy Hesseler, honorary counselor to the Cour des Monnaies in Lyons. He also undertook several embellishments: on the ground floor, he had bays with curved lintels made, while replacing the Renaissance portal and loggias with kitchens. Through marriage, the estate of Bagnols passed afterwards to the Croppet de Varissan family, then to the rich Montbellet de Saint-Try who replaced the ancient wall paintings with wood paneling. The château, which remained intact through the French Revolution, was put under seal in 1793. The following year, a barrister, Claude Marie Chavanis, purchased the château. Around 1820, his son converted the garden into a vineyard and vegetable garden. There were few modifications until the end of the nineteenth century, when the majestic fireplace in the Guards' Hall was restored by the Chavannes family, the château's owners until 1980.

The ancient Guards' Hall where guests dine facing one of France's most beautiful fireplaces, decorated with carved figures and angels bearing blazonry. Restored at the end of the nineteenth century, its central part is stamped with the escutcheon of France, a souvenir of Charles VIII's stay in 1490.

A masterpiece of Italian art: the sofa, carved from walnut, stands out clearly against the trompe l'oeil frescoes of the Grand Salon, with its architecture and frames on a background of silks.

Red damask, wood paneling, bright floor tiles, and an eighteenth-century bed are the dominant features of the Anne Dugné Suite. The bathroom is endowed with an Empire bathtub (right).

Enthroned in the middle of an eighteenth-century decor of painted wood paneling, a sumptuous Polish-style bed from the Louis XVI period lined with nineteenth-century brocaded silk. The period fireplaces work in every room (below).

Photo on pages 20 and 21:
Madame de Sévigné came to Bagnols in 1672 when it was owned by the Dugués. The decor in her suite, inspired by a sixteenth-century Italian motif, dates back to 1625. Her desk and harpsichord remained at the château for many years.

When the Hamlyns decided to revive the soul of the château in 1987, it was in complete disrepair: the roofing in the west wing had collapsed and a good number of the rooms, which had to be redistributed, were insalubrious. Doors had to be refitted, wood paneling removed, bathrooms created . . . all without allowing the practical aspect of their installation to harm the aesthetic of the whole. The Hamlyns' decision to pursue the renovation with restraint required artful techniques, as effective as they were discreet:. For example, the floor tiles had to be removed one by one in order to conceal kilometers of electric cables, the whole directed entirely by computer. This site, so rich in history and memories, subtly turned into a modern showcase. The restoration of the wall paintings alone took two years, mobilizing five teams of specialists. The people in the village of Bagnols, seeing such a far-reaching project come true, were most cooperative.

To furnish these rooms, Helen Hamlyn drew from her personal collections, or had copies made in England: a Polish-style bed, an Aix-style sofa inlaid with mutton bone, a bread cart inspired by the

A bathroom fitted out in a tower, with painted arcades from the early seventeenth century, is lit by a loop-hole, a window opening once intended for the château's defense. The two circular mirrors were brought back from England.

The washstands and taps in the bathrooms of the château.

Detail of the wall paintings done in 1630 in the Bouquet Suite, taking up the motifs on fabric, velvet, and damask inspired by those of the school of Lyons. Above, a bouquet on a pink background.

The seventeenth-century paintings in the ancient donjon evoke hunting scenes. Displaying the Mannerist style of late sixteenth-century prints, their backgrounds are treated in shadings of very pale blues and greens.

kind used by bakers of old, are just a few examples of her design selections. The abundant time allowed for the château's rehabilitation permitted her to think through every detail. The choice of textiles, stretched inside out to rediscover the mat finish of the fabric which only the patina of time can offer, comes from the same respect for history which presided over the arrangement of the gardens. Outlined with laser after eighteenth- and nineteenth-century inventories, they were replanted with yew and cherry trees a year before the hotel opened. The quality of the whole is in fact due to this exceptional woman who designed or adapted almost all of the hotel's everyday objects: from a breakfast service of Edwardian inspiration, emblazoned porcelain Limoges china, eighteenth-century Burgundy glasses recreated in Alsace, to bedding made specially in Switzerland with a quality of thread not found in France . . .

If you visit the Bouquet Suite, whose chimney mantelpiece recalls the arabesques on the walls, the small Hunt Room with its painted ceiling, or Gaspard Dugué's bedroom, where the apse of a chapel dedicated to Saint Jerome now serves as an alcove, the almost spiritual respect for authenticity—miles away from the pretentious reconstructions meant to "mark an era"—makes the restoration appear as if tapped by the magic wand of a fairy, the touch of a great English lady who has saved the château from a mortal sleep.

In this type of venture, money is not all that is required. More than a luxury hotel, Château de Bagnols asserts itself as an "altar of taste."

In the Madame de Sévigné Suite, a detail from the wall paintings—foliage scrolls within crowns framed by vases, out of which birds escape—set against a pink background.

CHÂTEAU DE PRUNOY

~

We have built a house that is not for Time's throwing.

Rupert Brooke

One of the two ponds that have not been drained on the estate. Man-made in the eighteenth century, the ponds are drained ritually, every five years, in the presence of the châtelaine (left).

The stately arrival to Château de Prunoy, framed by the foliage of its park, which measures one hundred hectares. With its Régence façade, its corner turrets, and its French-style gardens, Prunoy is among the landmark historical sites of the eighteenth century (below).

Certain residences are like some people. We come upon them by chance, without suspecting what a strong impression they will leave us with. Yet there is nothing grandiose about them; they have a distinguished air, which is exceptional in that it unites, in the same body, magnificence and a proper balance of all elements.

With its Régence façades girdled by square turrets, its elegant pediment, and its joyful alternation of bull's eye windows, dormers, and slender chimneys on its slate roof, Château de Prunoy, located on the outskirts of Burgundy between Courtenay and Auxerre, is without question a pure example of eighteenth-century French architecture. Its harmonious ensemble is enhanced by the infinite views that look out over a park of a hundred hectares (one hectare equals 2.47 acres). Designed by a student of the great seventeenth-century landscape designer André Le Nôtre, the park boasts wide lawns bordered by bountiful trees, romantic ponds glimpsed through a gap in the forest, a wooded path encircling the property. In these protected surround-ings, everything combines to create a unique visual effect.

The history of Château de Prunoy, run as a hotel by Josée Roumilhac since 1983, does not have a fairy tale beginning. In

Photos on pages 26 and 27:

Page 26: *On the garden side, half hidden by ivy, the old sixteenth-century bell near the entrance.*

Page 27: *Bearing the Lalive coat of arms, the superb pediment crowning the entry portal was carved in the early eighteenth century (top).*
Erected in the sixteenth century, this wooden campanile is located above the entry. Its clockwork is between the two suites on the second floor (bottom, left).
On the summit of the Renaissance tower, a sixteenth-century weather vane atop the ancient library (bottom, right).

Oh! there the chestnuts, summer through,
Beside the river make for you
A tunnel of green gloom, and sleep
Deeply above . . .

Rupert Brooke

the early sixteenth century, Guillaume Crèvecœur—son of Philippe Crèvecœur, who negotiated the celebrated treaty of Arras that reattached Burgundy to France—chose this site to build Château de Vienne. The estate, measuring three thousand hectares, was later owned by François Christophe de Lalive, the tax collector-general, who ordered the château razed in 1721. Today, only the round tower—called the library—and the magnificent framework remain of the original Gothic château. At Lalive's death in 1765, the property passed on to Ange Laurent Lalive de Jully, an artist and diplomat. Reconsidering the garden's lay-out, he increased the number of plants and drained its ponds. During the French Revolution, no physical damage was done to the main building, yet it had been abandoned as early as 1779. In 1826, the chapel burned down. The last of the Lalive family then sold the estate to a nephew, Raymond-Aymery, Duke of Montesquiou-Fezensac and French

The kitchen is in the oldest part of the main building. Arranged by the owner, it features a long table with colored ceramic tiles created by Yves Marthelot. On the wall, between the two windows, are painted wood panels with rustic motifs bordered by polychrome squares.

Bright and luminous, the large entry hall displays Régence wainscoting, decorations above the doors done by the eighteenth-century painter Jean-Baptiste Oudry, and a herring-bone parquet.

The soft comfort of the large drawing room: a Régence chandelier, windows masked by drapes, an antique Turkish carpet, deep armchairms, and wood fires.

ambassador to Madrid. Raymond-Aymery had the château restored in 1851. His daughter, Henriette Oriane, the wife of Count de Goyon, inherited the château and devoted herself to the revival of this historical site. Around 1900, the de Goyon family, in its turn, sold the property to Georges Raverat.

Raverat's son Jacques, who later married Charles Darwin's granddaughter, was one of the driving forces behind a group of English intellectuals baptized the "Neo-Pagans." Another leader was Rupert Chawner Brooke, the radiant poet whose glory was assured by his war sonnets. This movement, which grouped Bertrand Russell, André Gide, D. H. Lawrence, E. M. Forster, and Katherine Cox, did not survive World War I. But from 1910 to 1916 this talented community of writers met at Prunoy to pursue its dreams.

In 1917, after some bad financial speculations, Georges Raverat sold the estate. It was purchased by the Roumilhac family in 1926. During World War II, the Germans occupied Prunoy and afterward left with all its furniture. Josée Roumilhac was only twenty in 1955 when she inherited the "château of misery," by then overgrown with bushes. She opened the château to the public in 1971 to inaugurate the first "Court of Antiquarians" and a disco installed in the château's outbuildings.

In 1974, Prunoy was listed as a historical landmark. Seven years later, Josée de Roumilhac, until then an antique dealer in Paris, decided to live at the château and turn it into an inn-hotel.

The mistress of the manor, who is as warm as she is imaginative, has more than string in her bow. Not only is she an antique dealer and an excellent cook, she also possesses an unusual knack for managing grand sites. Since the early 1970s, the entire estate has been the site for numerous artistic, cultural, and sporting events. Prunoy has welcomed and celebrated many guests with numerous costumed balls, parties, and special events. Christmas eves spent around gigantic crèches and sideboards piled high with presents, hot-air

View of the hall leading to the Golden Salon. A Louis XVI console, placed under a Venetian mirror, holds up fragile chinoiseries.

Photo on pages 34 and 35:
Two pages, sculpted from wood and brought back from Portugal, have watched over the paneled hall since the eighteenth century.

The walls in the Isis Room are adorned with three panels painted in the Egyptian manner. The statuette representing bucolic love, once part of Alexandre Dumas's collection at Château de Monte Cristo, is now enthroned in front of one of the bay windows.

The "garden-style" corner bathroom in the Rose Room, arranged by Josée Roumilhac.

The Sunflower Suite in the Renaissance wing was recently redecorated. Its eclectic style, in yellow and black, reaches its apotheosis with the "banana armchair" designed by Yves Marthelot.

balloon rides in the park, and summer concerts featuring soloists and quartets are all part of the world of Prunoy. These are the rituals of modern-day court life; the traditions of a landowner, however, are also strictly observed. Every five years, the ponds are emptied in the presence of the châtelaine! Most of the festivities are held on the ground floor, whose decor is periodically renewed according to Josée de Roumilhac's finds: they take place on the Versailles parquet of the large, wood-paneled entrance hall, under the silent watch of two wood statues placed there like sentinels. In the large Régence drawing room with its gilt paneling, the sounds of footsteps are muffled by a genuine Turkish carpet. In the Petit Salon, the château's game room, lily petals fall on an exquisite chess set.

Château de Prunoy has two faces, simultaneously offering the charm of residences of yesteryear and the comforts and conveniences of modern living. Amenities include everything from a resort spa in the outbuildings and a turquoise swimming pool in the middle of a meadow to rooms outfitted as conference centers.

As for dining pleasure, the cuisine remains resolutely in the great tradition of fine French cooking.

The rooms that welcome our dreams have Roman names and a touch of legend. The Harmony Suite on the ground floor has five windows and an easel. On the first floor, the Azur Room has children's marionettes; the Rose Room, an exquisite corner bathroom furnished in rattan; the Sidonie, a Directoire single bed; and the Orpheus, eighteenth-century church wood. Still higher up, the Old Oak Suite holds up the massive frame of the ancient sixteenth-century tower. Thanks to the audacity of this medley of styles and the eclecticism of their arrangement, Château de Prunoy evokes those "cluttered-nest" family homes that each generation enriches with new curios. And new life.

The serpentine lines of the belle époque bathroom in the 1900 Suite, overlooking the large drive. This rare art nouveau ensemble is worthy of a museum.

La Mirande

~

*In the shadow of the Palais des Papes,
the stern residence of a cardinal is softened
by the splendor of the eighteenth century*

Photos on pages 38 and 39:

Page 38: *An "old manor" damask cushion on one of the upholstered divans, which is set against the striped taffeta wall tapestry of the Red Salon.*

Page 39: *The well-proportioned façade, attributed to Pierre Mignard. Pierre de Vervins ordered it built in 1688 on the site of Cardinal Arnaud de Pellegrue's former livery, which burned down during the siege of the Palais des Papes. The façade is listed as a historical landmark* (top).
On raised ground, one of the interior terraces that extend La Mirande's secret garden (bottom).

To get to the hotel's small terrace (above), guests cross this vestibule with wood paneling designed by the decorator François-Joseph Graf. The furniture, painted after an eighteenth-century Italian original, is arranged on a cement tile floor dating from the beginning of the century. Between the two windows adorned in percale by the firm of le Manach, a portrait by Jean Béraud.

Other than a well-known bridge and a no less prestigious theater festival, Avignon has an ancient quarter where the members of the Sacred College settled in the fourteenth century, the period when the city was the papal see. Built on the Place de la Mirande, in the shadow of the Palais des Papes (Palace of the Popes), between the orchard of Urban V and the church of Saint Peter, the mansion was formerly owned by the Pamard family. Converted in 1990 into an opulent hotel-restaurant, the site has a rich history.

More than six hundred years ago, Cardinal Arnaud de Pellegrue, a nephew of Pope Clement V, installed his livery in an ensemble of buildings erected on the remnants of a Roman villa. Only a small staircase in the court and some vestiges in the cellars remain from this period. The handsome edifice of today was not built until 1688, when it was commissioned by Pierre de Vervins, the procurator-general for the pope. Pierre de Vervins had La Mirande's noble façade built in the most pure Louis XIV style, following plans by Pierre Mignard. During the French Revolution, the house belonged to the Marquise de Lattier who remained the sole owner until her death. Her heirs sold it on October 21, 1796, to Jean-Baptiste Pamard, a health officer. The mansion remained in his family for two hundred years before becoming, in 1987, the property of Achim and Hannelore Stein. While respecting the site's eventful history, the Steins adapted its intimate spirit as a private residence to the highly cosmopolitan tone required by a luxury hotel.

Responding to the majesty of its

Adjoining the rear of the Palais des Papes, the garden—planted with chestnut trees, weeping willows, and laurels—reveals its secret as it leads to La Mirande's two interior terraces.

For a breakfast safe from prying eyes, a glade in the secret garden shaded by tall chestnut trees.

The formal perfection of the Louis XIV door knocker decorating the entry door.

ensemble, Achim Stein had only one wish: to restore La Mirande to its eighteenth-century splendor. After a year of research and reflection came two years of renovation under the direction of Gilles Grégoire, an architect from Avignon who specializes in the art of restoration; François-Joseph Graf, a renowned decorator from Paris; and the owners' son, Martin Stein, who attentively followed each restructuring phase of this exceptional landmark.

The Steins had to do more than just restore a decor that would be reverential and historically irreproachable. They also had to refind, and at the same time re-create, the unique climate of a residence where past styles could mix harmoniously without allowing the reconstruction effort to alter its irreplaceable atmosphere. The Steins sought to render the spirit of a "house with character," offered by homes that have been inhabited continuously for generations and which reflect the owners' love and diversity of tastes. Calling on their own knowledge and sensibility as well as on the experience of skilled artisans, the Steins have succeeded in giving La Mirande this rare sense of personality.

In order to suggest the apartment suites in enfilade of the eighteenth century, the couple hired carpenters to fashion wainscoting using false doors. Blacksmiths, basing their work on a model at Château de Barbentane, re-created a superb banister for the main staircase that leads to the upper floor. (The staircase has replaced an

A small masterpiece in the Red Salon: a terra-cotta statuette by Jean-Baptiste Carpeaux representing the spirit of dance, placed on a Provençal console of gilded wood and marble. Behind the statuette, the mirror reflects the eighteenth-century chandelier and the wall tapestry.

At the bar's entrance opening onto the patio, antique furniture re-created in Italy.

The warm, plush atmosphere of the bar: its wall hangings are the work of the tapestry-maker Phelippeau; the sofa is covered in a printed cloth created by the firm of le Manach.

earlier one designed by the celebrated nineteenth-century architect Viollet-le-Duc.) To avoid disturbing the beauty of a double-caisson ceiling from the fifteenth century, the decor painters worked patiently on the patina of the walls in the immense dining room.

Without pretentious exoticism or absurd historicism, the furnishings at La Mirande cross time as well as space: all of the tapestries were woven after antique French cartoons; the various copies of period furniture come from Italy; the bedding in the rooms—which differ in all aspects except the prettiness of their proportions—and the taps in the bathrooms come from Great Britain; the carpets, from Baghdad; the light fixtures, from Zurich. The decided taste for period chairs, for wood repainted in light colors, and for the recurrent use of a potted shrub design, are borrowed from the highly civilized culture of Provence. Together these styles create a refined restoration which, since La Mirande presents itself as a simple and welcoming residence, does not intimidate anyone by its virtuosity.

While arousing a certain artistic zeal, this sophisticated retreat has the magic power to make those who stay here forget that a hotel is, above all, a place of passage. La Mirande is a peerless hotel that can be appreciated as the

The dining room, whose fifteenth-century caisson ceiling is listed as a historical landmark, required a decor of high quality. Tables covered with heavily pleated tablecloths are set up on a large carpet done in petit point by nuns at the end of the nineteenth century. Above the well-proportioned fireplace, a work by the Provençal painter Bergier.

François-Joseph Graf designed his decor entirely around the fifteen Chinese wallpaper panels from the eighteenth century. In the foreground, set on an antique rug, armchairs upholstered in printed cotton with a "Montgolfière" (fire-balloon) motif designed by Pierre Frey. The fabric was stretched on the reverse side to give the armchairs an antique look.

This large staircase, whose wrought-iron banister was inspired by one at Château de Barbentane, replaced the earlier staircase which was designed according to plans by the nineteenth-century architect Viollet-le-Duc.

consummate project of enlightened amateurs and not as the private museum of hoteliers/art patrons who want to be considered archaeologists of taste as well.

Seconded by the talent of François-Joseph Graf, the Steins, while insinuating a variety of references in their decors, searched for textiles and wallpapers capable of enhancing the size and ambience of the rooms. From Venice to London they scoured tirelessly for furniture and curios that would evoke a noteworthy aesthetic accent to the antique tile flooring and blown glass windows.

To grasp the scope of such an undertaking, you only need to let yourself be taken in by the distinctive atmosphere of each room. The interior court, covered by a glass roof and furnished with delicately painted wicker armchairs and potted shrubs, could easily be mistaken for a winter garden. Arranged around the court, the ten rooms on the ground floor include the famous Crimson Salon that evokes the interior of a theater. Its

showpiece is a terra-cotta statuette by the nineteenth-century sculptor Jean-Baptiste Carpeaux, representing the spirit of dance, set on a Provençal console of gilded wood and marble. The drawing room reflects the style of two eras with its Napoleon III furniture and dimensions and its precious Louis XV chimneypiece and chandelier.

But there is no doubt that the Chinese salon holds the greatest interest. Here, François-Joseph Graf, with an expert decorative eloquence, created an unprecedented space and decor, designed around fifteen Chinese wallpaper panels dating from the eighteenth century.

A number of masterpieces are brilliantly assembled in the large dining room. This room, with its Renaissance ceiling with double caissons, is listed as a historical treasure along with La Mirande's seventeenth-century façade. A d'Aubusson tapestry entitled *The Collation* hangs on the wall, and on the floor lies an immense carpet woven by

Isolated in the embrasure of one of the windows in Room 27, the delicate grace of a small chaise longue, glorified by the opulence of silk taffeta curtains created by le Manach.

Photo on pages 48 and 49:
The large glass case in the small private dining room protects an antique porcelain collection. Here, guests enjoy intimate dinner parties at the table once used by the Pamard family.

nuns at the end of the nineteenth century. An exquisite antique porcelain collection can be admired in the small private dining room, where guests dine on the table once used by the Pamard family.

The bar, which offers a gallery of delicate portraits, leads to the unexpected exuberance of a secret garden. In this oasis of calm you can let your eyes slide over the proud bareness of the nearby Palais des Papes' chalky walls, and when you have adjusted to their spare beauty, you can then look back at the interior of the hotel and better appreciate, once again, the rich detail, handsome antiques, flowered percales, and deep tonalities.

The private guest rooms, whose decor is treated more soberly than the public rooms, are also paneled and feature chambranles and lintels. In keeping with the layout of classical architecture, they are wider on the top floor than on the second. Two of the rooms have a small terrace that overlooks the roofs of Avignon.

La Mirande is more than just a hotel. Thanks to the competence and discreet vigilance of Martin Stein, lovingly watches over this remarkable establishment, it has not succumbed to provincial languor. The hotel sponsors a number of artistic events, holding art exhibits in the magnificent vaulted cellars and chamber music concerts in the vast dining room. Another of the hotel's strong points: catering prepared by a large staff directed by Chef Eric Loitel.

The charms of life have not vanished in Avignon. Miraculously, La Mirande, a cultural center pleasing all the senses, offers more than luxury; here, voluptuousness reigns.

All in arabesques, the pretty, old-fashioned charm of the small balcony in Room 36, overlooking the roofs of Avignon.

On the first floor, Provençal harmonies in the most luminous corner of Room 20. Fabrics by Braquenié. The bathroom features a partition typical of nineteenth-century Avignon decors.

The corner drawing room of Room 34, on the top floor, is organized around the "cul-de-four" window. The room's rich motifs are emphasized by the wallpaper samples framed on the walls.

"The charm of this mirror is that it lends me its beauty."

Discovered in a secondhand shop, this magnifying mirror, dating most likely from the nineteenth century, plays a leading role in the decor of the bathroom in Room 29.

In the bathroom of La Mirande's only suite, wallpaper with a trompe l'oeil drapery effect from the firm of Mauny. The washstands and taps, direct from England, are from the firms of Hart and Adam & Sons.

Château de Remaisnil

~

The art of life à la française
revisited by Laura Ashley

Photos on pages 54 and 55:

Page 54: *View from the court side: the former stables, today converted into a conference center, and the château's dovecote.*

Page 55: *View from the garden side: Château de Remaisnil, seen through the opening in its alley of hundred-year-old oaks. The façade is in a pure rococo style of the late eighteenth century.*

Bushes and clumps of flowers in the English-style garden. The owners' Anglo-Saxon origins are most clearly expressed in the château's park.

Detail of the greenhouse built at the beginning of the century. Today, grapes are grown there.

An adventure usually begins as soon as we leave our regular surroundings. For the Doulls, who find themselves today in the middle of the Picardy countryside in the north of France, at the head of this ancestral château, it is definitely a matter of adventure—because nothing prepared the couple (he is South African, she is American) for their life as châtelains, and even less for their new vocation as hoteliers.

This modern fairy tale began in the spring of 1987. At that time, Adrian Doull held an important post with a large American mining company, and his wife, Susan, was an executive at a major bank. They lived with their two children in New York. On a business flight to London, Adrian Doull's attention was drawn to an article in the Sunday Telegraph: Château de Remaisnil, the property of the celebrated designer Laura Ashley, was up for sale. Why did he feel the desire to know more? Some secret attraction, some impulse? But there he was, having crossed the Channel, scouring the Picardy countryside in search of the famous château, without even knowing where it was located. And then, at a bend in the road, through a vista created by an alley of hundred-year-old oaks, he finally discovered the château. It was love at first sight. Three months later, he had purchased it.

Château de Remaisnil has spanned several centuries, not without chaos, and nearly risked not being built at all. Construction began in 1760 under the impetus of Théodore de la Porte and his wife, Henriette de Wintershove, of the house of Flanders. Unfortunately, the French Revolution was to destroy a large part of the structures already built. Théodore's son, Jean-Joseph, who was born at Remaisnil in 1762, took up the project again a years later, after the revolutionary turmoil had ended. He himself had survived the war by living in the area as a simple peasant, and changing his aristocratic name to the more ordinary name of Laporte. The residence

Soaring up from the roof of the outbuildings, the campanile recalls the watchtowers, set over mines and slag heaps, that once dominated the countryside of northern France.

Photo on pages 58 and 59:
*The large drawing room restored by Laura Ashley,
the château's former owner. The chandelier, carpets,
furniture, lamps, and candelabras are period
furnishings; the curtains were designed by Laura Ashley.*

he erected is the one we see today: a main building with a central forepart and two wings at a slight return, the whole capped by a mansard roof.

With its rococo style, of neoclassical Louis XVI construction, Château de Remaisnil belongs to the tradition of eighteenth-century Picardy architecture. Built with local materials, bricks, and chalk, its somewhat austere façade was embellished with friezes and the owner's armorial medallions. At the entrance to the park, the former stables, converted today into a conference center and rooms, appear more sober, topped by a sort of campanile which recalls the watchtowers that were erected at one time between the slag heaps and mines further north, in the French mining region. Time seems to stop as soon as you enter the château. Everything contributes to perpetrate this illusion: the creak of the ancient parquet, the subtle interplay of mirrors only slightly tarnished by the years, immense wall tapestries, Aubusson carpets, fireplaces where logs crackle, and most of all, the impressive crystal chandeliers lighting each room. Remaisnil may have changed hands many times, but its successive owners knew how to respect its identity, including Laura Ashley who, better than anyone, succeeded in enhancing this historical landmark with her well-known taste and ingenuity.

In the mid 1970s, she began a true work of restoration. The entire decor—the mostly Louis XVI furniture, the imposing crystal lamps over the period pedestal tables, the hangings that drape over the windows—was faithfully recreated, not with pale copies but by using ancient and noble materials. The library,

*The small drawing room, blending Louis XVI and
Directoire furniture.*

*In the billiard room, the eighteenth-century
billiard table is as old as the château itself.*

*Done in shades of green, the library displays wood
moldings and friezes unique in the north of France.*

done in shades of green, splendidly illustrates this, with painted wood paneling and carvings that are unique in the north of France. And in the new rooms, outfitted for her own comfort, the designer took care to use period furniture, as in the billiard room, where the striking billiard table is as old as the château itself.

Château de Remaisnil became Laura Ashley's principal residence, serving as the rallying point for her design teams, which were scattered all over the world. In order to receive them royally, she appointed each room as an exquisite haven of peace. The Doulls, the new owners, wisely did not change these subtle arrangements, which today offer guests a level of comfort and an art of living almost unique among French hotels. The addition of several bathrooms was the only sacrifice granted to modern life. As for the rest of the decor, each room is carefully differentiated, as initially designed by Laura Ashley herself: the Ritz Room is tapestried with a fabric patterned after a model she discovered in the renowned Paris hotel; the Louis XVI Room features period furniture and a canopied bed, and the impressive Napoleon Room is decorated with stretched fabrics like a vast field tent.

Situated in the heart of one of France's oldest regions, Château de Remaisnil has been justly designated as a historical landmark. But, thanks to the grace created by Laura Ashley and to the warm welcome which the Doulls offer their guests, we recognize, when we are at the château, how much history is what people make of it.

The Laura Ashley touch can be sensed even in the corridors that lead to the rooms; it is particularly noticeable in the drape of the curtains adorning the windows.

In the Louis XVI room, the period furniture is in perfect harmony with the fabrics designed by Laura Ashley.

The Ritz Room owes its name to a fabric designed by Laura Ashley, patterned after a model originating from the renowned hotel in Paris.

GRAND HÔTEL NORD PINUS

~

"En Arles où sont les Alyscamps
prend garde à la douceur des choses."

Paul-Jean Toulet

Photos on pages 64 and 65:

Page 64: Nightfall on the Place du Forum. The hotel's electric signs are lit, crowning the two high windows of the façade under a garland of rounded tiles.

Page 65: The opulent beauty of richly brocaded fabrics; their exquisite motifs evoke the suit of lights worn by toreadors (top). Shaded by chestnut trees, the modest façade of the hotel built on top of an ancient Roman cryptoporticus. The long balcony crossing its width belongs to Room 10, once reserved for toreadors (bottom).

The hotel's strange name, underscored by the Provençal writer Jean Giono, is not the only thing that is eccentric about the Nord Pinus. The former Grand Hôtel du Nord—the shrine of high society "belonging to the memory of all the people of Arles," according to the fashion designer Christian Lacroix—is probably protected by the city's ancient forum gods as well as by the ghost of the toreador Luis-Miguel Dominguin.

Founded at the end of the nineteenth century by a Monsieur Pinus, the establishment, which at that time was modest, fell to the Bessières family and was inherited by one of their descendants, Nello, the famous tightrope walker of the Medrano Circus. But it was his wife Germaine, an ex-cabaret dancer with a strong personality and extravagant habits, who was, by all accounts, its high priestess. Today, it is yet another woman, Anne Igou, who reigns there. The owner since 1987, she has considerably improved the hotel's comfort, and the Nord Pinus is currently renewing its past tradition as a fashionable hotel.

Except for the evident traces of the Roman cryptoporticus on which the hotel was built, the building's history is rather obscure. At first you see only a provincial façade overlooking the Place du Forum. The square, formerly named Place des Hommes, bears a statue of Frédéric Mistral, the nineteenth-century Provençal writer, with its back turned to the hotel.

A long, wrought-iron balcony crosses the width of the hotel's façade. The balcony belongs to Room 10, reserved for prominent guests and for toreadors: after one memorable corrida, Dominguin,

A corner of the hall-salon. The large wrought-iron staircase, rising upwards, leads to the rooms. Some wardrobe trunks, placed near the bottom steps, symbolize this bohemian hotel, which was, in the early 1950s, the obligatory stopping-off place for many celebrities who traveled to the south of France.

The hotel entrance, opening onto the salon and the reception desk. Before dining in town, guests enjoy lingering, glass in hand, in one of the tawny, leather easy chairs.

The hall-salon recalls a chapel dedicated to music. In the background, one of the wrought-iron chandeliers decorated with a boat, chosen for the hotel by Nello and Germaine Bessières. The decor includes kitsch and a fountain in a harmony of brown and red.

Against one of the salon walls, three magnificent fashion photographs by Peter Lindberg, placed like a retable above an altar cluttered with relics and souvenirs.

The hotel's stairwell. When the hotel became the property of bankruptcy trustees, the wrought-iron banister remained the exclusive property of Germaine Bessières.

In "Le Cintra," the bar's poster collection and other bullfighting icons celebrate the rituals of the corridas, as well as those of the ferias.

Photos on pages 68, 69, and 70:

Pages 68 and 69: *The bar "Le Cintra" has a decor dedicated entirely to bullfighting: a suit of lights in a showcase, the mounted head of a bull, and a Virgin of Rosio. "Le Cintra" is the rendezvous for notable guests and for devotees of Arles' nightlife.*

Page 70: *Behind the bar, the aficionados' corner, characterized by a series of black-and-white photographs retracing the great moments in the hotel's history: matadors such as Dominguin dressed in the suit of lights, and artists of every discipline, including Cocteau, Picasso, and Yves Montand.*

spotted with blood, stood on the balcony to receive an ovation from the crowd below. Arles, through which the Rhône flows, is a city of ancient fifth-century amphitheaters. The hotel, near these bullfighting arenas, is a favorite with matadors, and its bar, "Le Cintra," has a decor entirely devoted to tauromachy, displaying a suit of lights, the mounted head of a bull, posters from corridas, and other bullfighting icons.

The hotel had its hour of glory after World War II: it became an obligatory pilgrimage for every celebrity who traveled to the south of France. In its heyday, the Arles hotel was frequented regularly by Jean Cocteau and Ernest Hemingway. The hotel's astounding guest register, begun in 1927 by the Prince of Bourbon-Parma and Henri de Régnier, bears witness to this glory. The guests included many writers, but also painters (such as Pierre de Chavannes and Picasso), actors (Sacha Guitry and Peter O'Toole), singers (Toni Rossi and Charles Trenet), and sports figures (Gianni Motta and Tomi Simpson).

Crowned heads, as well as political leaders, also numbered among its guests: figuring in the midst of hundreds of signatures are the names of King Farouk and Winston Churchill. The famous guest album also displays two delightful drawings: the Place du Forum sketched by Christian Bérard, and a dreamlike landscape imagined by Paul Klee.

Other than toreadors and their aficionados, Nello and Germaine Bessières, who were a rather bohemian couple, enjoyed having circus artists stay at their hotel. Dazzling evening parties and wild card games were common occurrences until Nello died in 1969. Germaine, prostrate with grief, suddenly lost interest in managing the hotel, which then went into a total collapse. Every object of value was sold to pay wages, and soon bankruptcy trustees seized the hotel. Abandoned by her clientele, Germaine nevertheless continued to lead a whimsical lifestyle until the early 1980s—bathing in algae until early afternoon; passing the days by the hotel's front door in summer; and, in winter, moving her living quarters into the hotel's large hall.

In 1987, she finally agreed to a takeover bid from Anne Igou, who, having given up her profession as a biologist, had decided to settle in the south of France. Germaine died a few days later, leaving the young woman a moldy building, a roof in ruin, and an unpaid bill for several large, wrought-iron beds she had ordered from the local blacksmith. The Nord Pinus still has some

Warmth and simplicity in the Provençal dining room, with blue-and-white checked tablecloths.

*The unique clientele at Grand Hôtel Nord Pinus:
stars of the bullring, divas of the opera, and the
leading lights of French haute coutre*

*The guest rooms, each painted a different color,
exude personalized comfort and gaiety.*

*Baroque console and frame in gilded wood in
the Matador Suite. Luis-Miguel Dominguin,
Montserrat Caballé, and Alexandre Lagoya
have stayed here.*

photographs showing the dilapidated rooms painted in loud colors. After a long delay, Anne Igou obtained a loan and then began the renovation. In the hall-vestibule, she kept the same pastel colors and the same wrought-iron chandeliers decorated with boats, adding several large, tawny, leather easy chairs and some trunks. In the rooms, which were still fresh-looking, she had the beds re-covered with white piqué. The newly tiled bathrooms were enlarged, and she had gigantic posters from Spanish corridas, collected by Christian Vial , placed on the walls.

Reopened in September of 1989, Grand Hôtel Nord Pinus again lives to the beat of the city's ferias—though today art and photography exhibits have replaced the card games.

More than a hotel, the Nord Pinus is a family home: that of the ancient kingdom of Arles. More than a historical site, it is a gallery of curios where crosses and Mexican good-luck charms are placed side by side with framed scarfs. Christian Lacroix has a room here; pale blue, it overlooks the impasse. Other guest rooms are colored in soft pink and lilac. The Matador Suite, in the style of Napoleon III , regularly welcomes the diva Montserrat Caballé and Alexandre Lagoya. Going back down the large wrought-iron staircase to return to the bar "Le Cintra," one of the altars of Arles' nightlife, three words come to mind to define the Nord Pinus: simplicity, authenticity, and uniqueness.

*One of the fresh-looking rooms ornamented
with ancient Provençal boutis and piqués, discovered by Anne Igou in antique shops. The
wrought-iron beds were ordered by Germaine
Bessières from the local blacksmith.*

Le Rosier

~

The secret opulence of Flemish mansions

What better recognition for a hotel than to become so unique that it is considered an absolute point of reference? After only twenty years, this is the amazing destiny in store for Rosier. Originally simply called Rosier, after its location on the rue Rosier, in the heart of Antwerp's historic quarter, the hotel has henceforth become "Le" Rosier. Unrivaled, it is incontestably the most beautiful hotel in the Belgian city, if not one of the most charming in the world, according to Harpers & Queen's *Top 100 Best Hotels of the World*. This success is the achievement of three men, three close friends who have known each other for ages but whose respective professions certainly hadn't prepared them for the hotel trade. Besides, that was not their intent when they embarked on this adventure in 1972, after buying this ancient seventeenth-century family mansion. It had been occupied by nuns who had come from Africa to spend their remaining days, thanks to the kindness of the building's legal owner, a former governor of the Belgian Congo. Théo Bonné, a publicist; Walter De Bie, a business executive; and Bob Claes, an antiques dealer, all natives of Antwerp, fell in love at first sight with this makeshift convent. They acquired it not

Photos on pages 74 and 75:

Page 74: *Across the Orangerie, a glimpse of the Pompeian swimming pool furnished with painted wood seats and Roman busts.*

Page 75: *The hotel's interior garden, laid out in the French style by Jacques Wirtz. The fountain basins and statues add a Renaissance touch* (top).
The statue of Brabo "throwing the hand," the symbol for Antwerp's name and for its independence (bottom).

A statue of an ephebe, evidence of the exquisite taste and astonishing blend of neoclassical furnishings, which constitute the essential elements of Le Rosier's decoration.

The covered swimming pool, arranged and decorated to make it a true haven for relaxation (right).

In the private salon of the Orangerie: a harmony of blue and fawn colors, trompe l'oeil wood paneling, and an antique chandelier whose duplicate can only be found at the royal palace in Brussels (below).

Photo on pages 78 and 79:
The Medici Salon, the hotel's showplace, displays Le Rosier's most precious suite of furniture: armchairs after Jacob, an Aubusson carpet from the Charles X period, and a Beckstein piano.

only to live here, but also to welcome a handful of privileged guests and their friends.

From the beginning, Le Rosier was not conceived as an ordinary hotel but as a guest house. The three friends set up their own living quarters and then undertook considerable renovations to furnish the rooms and suites. To stay here is to be welcomed by friends who are always attentive and who respect the independence of their guests. And since each is unique, the rooms have been arranged and decorated as singular, distinctive premises. Guests who stay regularly at the hotel like to find these rooms again and again on their repeat visits, as if Le Rosier were for them a second home.

The three friends put their souls into this house, decorated by Bob Claes. Pursuing his activities as an antiques dealer, he was put in charge of the furnishings. Over the years, Le Rosier has come to resemble an antiques store where your eye is ceaselessly drawn by treasures heaped up according to some exquisite order and taste. Thus, furniture and decorations from the neoclassical period, which Bob Claes particularly favors, are set next to chinoiseries whose gilded blacks sparkle with light.

Built in a U-shape around the French-style garden, enhanced by an Italian

Detail from the Orangerie, revealing a deliberate quest for unity in the Restoration style.

Renaissance touch by the landscape gardener Jacques Wirtz, Le Rosier suggests a small château whose every wing has a function. The oldest part houses the "noble" quarters. On the ground floor, the flamboyant Medici Salon, all red and gold, features a splendid Aubusson carpet from the Charles X period. On the first floor, the "Siècle d'Or" Suite celebrates Antwerp's greatest period of prosperity, the "golden century" from the sixteenth to the seventeenth century. Furnished with antiques of the period, this suite, with its windows of small, colored, square panes, has preserved the charm of old Flemish houses. It was in this large room that the nuns once had their chapel and sacristy.

The central part of Le Rosier opens into the dining room, furnished in early American style, and onto a veranda-terrace. On inclement days, Antwerp's high society gathers here to drink tea while admiring the majestic biloba tree that spreads its branches over the garden. The other wing houses the Orangerie and Bob Claes's private salon, where guests may admire the antique chandelier and the trompe l'oeil wainscoting. Discreetly set, half hidden by a tapestry, a door permits access from there to the Pompeian-style swimming pool, decorated with wall paintings, painted wood seats, and Roman busts. By making a reservation, the fortunate guest can lounge here in solitude, protecting his privacy—as if he were at home.

As luck would have it, Antwerp's old prison stands only a hundred meters away, on the same rue Rosier. To remind us, no doubt, that hell is never very far from heaven. . .

Photos on pages 82 and 83:
The photographs on this page and opposite are of the "Siècle d'Or" Suite in the oldest part of the hotel. The suite once housed a chapel and a sacristy.

Seventeenth-century wrought iron and windows with small square panes in the Flemish tradition.

Furniture from Antwerp's golden age, dating from its period of expansion during the sixteenth and seventeenth centuries.

Detail of the original beams, decorated and carved.

The furnishings reflect Antwerp's prosperity during the time of Rubens, Van Dyck, Jordaens, and Plantin.

This massive wood chambranle once separated the chapel from the sacristy, converted today into a bathroom.

CASA DE CARMONA

~

"Oh, qu'il me soit donné, encore une fois,
de revoir quelques endroits aimés,
comme la Place du Pacifique à Séville."

Valery Larbaud

Photos on pages 84 and 85:

Page 84: *The first floor of Casa de Carmona, overlooking the central patio. The families who lived here used to spend the winter on the first floor, then move to the ground floor in summer.*

Page 85: *Streaming water, whether in a fountain or in the hotel's swimming pool, is the first sound that greets visitors to Casa de Carmona (top). From the exterior, nothing lets you guess that behind this sixteenth-century façade you will find the pinnacle of luxury and voluptuousness offered by modern comforts (bottom).*

The play of shadow and light sets off the walls' traditional colors, created from a base of lime and natural pigments.

The universe of Casa de Carmona is interior, even reclusive. Situated in the heart of Carmona, one of the oldest towns in Spain, the hotel as seen from the street only appears to be an aristocratic sixteenth-century dwelling, but without any ramparts, park, or even private drives. Who could suspect that the building is the temple of luxury and good taste in this ancestral land near Seville? From the outside, you might just be aware that for more than five centuries the house belonged to one of the most important dynasties in Andalusia, the Lasso de Vega family, which gave Spain many literary and political figures.

When you enter Casa de Carmona, you are in for a total surprise. Immediately, your attention is drawn by the discreet but reassuring presence of water—whether running in fountains or standing still in Casa de Carmona's long and narrow swimming pool, shaded by an immense palm tree. The sound of these streaming waters, audible in each interior court, has a lulling effect on even the busiest person. And you need only lift up your eyes to be impressed by the succession of arches and vaults whose every component has been preserved in the antique style. Everything—ochre fountains, burnt sienna walls, dusky brown statues, bronze and green monochrome armchairs, potted palms, slim cypresses, and orange trees—endeavors to remind you of nature as if these courts were a sort of interior garden meant to throw the brilliant blue of the sky into relief.

As has been done in every ancient Andalusian house in the region for ages, Casa de Carmona is organized around the central patio, embellished by a fountain and by a multitude of small potted box trees aligned in battle formation. Also according to tradition, there are actually two houses in one. The first, the vivienda alta (the high house), was once intended for winter use, whereas the second, the vivienda baja (the low house), usually welcomed the family in summer. Lifestyles may well have changed, but Casa de Carmona tries to respect ancestral customs: the reception desk, drawing rooms, and dining room, forming the hotel's common rooms, remain on the ground floor, while the more intimate rooms are on the first floor, reached by an impressive staircase decorated with azulejos, the small, blue-enameled, faience tiles of varying sizes that are so typically Iberian.

At Casa de Carmona, no one is ever received like an ordinary guest, even if one at a luxury hotel. One who stays at Casa de Carmona becomes the guest of Señora Medina, about whom everyone speaks with enthusiasm, admiration, and respect. Bold—

As in every Spanish house, the windows of Casa de Carmona are protected; some are also shielded by "guardapolvo," dust guards.

Every element in this series of vaults has been preserved in the antique style, including their coatings and colors.

her friends call her *atrevida* (a daredevil)—Marta Medina has succeeded in everything she has set out to do: from her start as a clothing designer at age eighteen, when she was creating ravishing outfits for herself; to her talent as an interior decorator, which she puts to use at her hotel; and including her life as a dashing woman of the world, which she carries off with brio in the Spanish capital.

Casa de Carmona is the ultimate expression of her multiple gifts. No professional decorator assisted her during the three years of work required for the building's complete restoration, after it had been neglected for decades. This is no doubt the secret for the hotel's extraordinary success: Marta Medina has invested a part of her soul in Casa de Carmona, thus creating a bewitching, and rather uncommon, impression. Guests who visit often feel as if they were in her home, although absolutely everything, down to the last detail, has been done to make them feel at home.

Many of the hotel's touches illustrate this art of living, created by civility and by

The Chess Salon, leading to the patio. The salon's objets d'art attest to the full life led by Casa de Carmona's proprietor, Señora Medina.

Photo on pages 90 and 91:
*The salon-library offers intimacy and the elegant jumble
of collectibles characteristic of opulent interiors.*

*Every lantern,
glass, and household
object is marked
with the seal of
Casa de Carmona.*

*Even the shutters, with hinged leaves, have been
restored to their original style.*

*Typically Iberian azulejos,
small, blue-enameled, faience
tiles of varying sizes, deck
the main staircase.*

a certain rigor mingled with a great nobility of bearing, which are typically Spanish character traits. Every sheet and pillowcase is embroidered and ironed by hand; every shower curtain is made of glazed chintz; every comforter is matched with the room's armchairs and curtains; every glass and sconce is engraved with two letter Cs topped by a crown, the stamp, indeed the very seal, of the Casa of Señora Medina.

Each room radiates a particular atmosphere, none resembling any other, up to and including their interior architecture. In one room are some canopied beds; in another, a staircase; elsewhere, a bathroom is subtly imbricated into a room by the effect of curtained French windows. Throughout the hotel one can also find an infinite variety of shimmering fabrics, delicate paintings, charming engravings above each bed, or the mahogany chest of drawers and restful chaise longues used for daily siestas, all of which ornament the salons of the "special" rooms. Not to be forgotten are the antique tiles that make up Casa de Carmona's original flooring, warmed by thick carpets from the Royale factory of Madrid.

A bar, permanently installed on a mahogany sideboard in one of the three salons in enfilade that open onto the central patio, offers a variety of liquor and soda bottles. Besides these standards, the sideboard is stocked with ice cubes, grilled almonds, and orange and lemon slices, all available to decorate cocktails or any other drink which you may prepare for yourself, and at your discretion—because that is how Señora Medina likes to entertain in her own home in Madrid.

When the sun burns brightly outside, Casa de Carmona offers a pleasant stroll through cool, shady courtyards

This door with caissons provides access to Señora Medina's private apartment. Her quarters also serve as Casa de Carmona's presidential suite.

Every arch in the hotel has been reinforced. The tile floors, dating from the sixteenth century, were relaid after being removed to install pipes and conveniences.

Detail of the presidential suite's frieze and its midnight blue ceiling, studded with stars (right).

Señora Medina's private apartment (and presidential suite). Though guests may have the impression of being in her house, everything has been designed to make them feel at home (below).

You get the same sense of intimacy when you see a picture frame set on some piece of furniture. The photos evoke Senora Medina's personal souvenirs, but far from seeming immodest, they give you a feeling of well-being, the sort ordinarily experienced only in the home of a loved one.

The young women on staff, whom you might cross coming around a hall corner, wear appealing, flounced aprons. All natives of Carmona, they were trained by a lady who belongs to the high society in Seville. For two months, she taught them how to move without making noise, how to respond to the wishes of each guest, how to grant their slightest whims with a smile, and even how to pack their bags (if that is their desire) wearing a pair of white gloves. Every six months, the "professor" returns to lavish on them new and valuable advice. Could anyone dream of any better training than this home-made apprenticeship? The concierge and gardener, who worked on Casa de Carmona's masonry during the renovation, consider this house their masterpiece and perform their new duties with pride.

Señora Medina returns to the hotel on average about once a month, usually for the weekends. She stays in her private apartment: two rooms and an immense

"Il faut avoir de l'âme pour avoir du goût."
Vauvenargues

Richly brocaded curtains, moiré armchairs, azulejos; each room is a harmony of colors and materials. Each room's decoration and architecture is distinct and unique.

Luxury even in the bathrooms, where the curtains are of glazed chintz and the taps and plumbing are of the best English make.

Though every room has its own cachet, all the beds are draped by the Compagnie des Indes, and all the sheets are ironed by hand.

drawing room filled with rare objects, deep sofas, comfortable armchairs, and, crowning all, a superb grand piano. Located on the first floor of the hotel, her private apartment serves as the presidential suite (with two cats you can rent, too!) after she leaves again, either for Madrid or for London where she buys most of the hotel's furniture and fabrics, up to and including the gleaming plumbing in the antique bathrooms. In fact, the Casa is like an Iberian "cork," concealing British treasures. And you will find numerous catalogues from Sotheby's and Christie's carelessly "lying around" in the rooms and in the reading salons on the ground floor. In these salons reign intimacy and the elegant, jumbled characteristic that results when opulent interiors overflow with collectibles bearing witness to a life fully lived.

Every day at Casa de Carmona is punctuated by the *vela*, a large canvas sailcloth which is drawn over the central patio by ten o'clock in the morning. Orange colored and pierced with tiny pinholes, the *vela* traces a pattern on the ground with each passing hour, its small lozenges of light moving like so many stars illuminating a summer sky. The light and the magic that settle over the patio give the

walls surprising depths and surfaces—a strange sight, indeed the same sensation you might have felt as a child, looking out at the world through the wrapping paper of an orange candy. This "acidulated" light protects guests from the dangerous effects of the sun until nightfall.

During these afternoon hours, Casa de Carmona maintains a pleasant tranquility, inviting guests to abandon themselves to the refreshing siesta practiced by every Andalusian during the hot season. And when the belfry of the nearby cathedral rings six o'clock, and the main square of the village begins to come to life again, Casa de Carmona wakes up, too. The *vela* is rolled back and the stars appear. Those up in the celestial vault will also mark, in their transit, the passage of time. The patio arc-lamps are lit, at a stroke rendering the ochers more pastel. Casa de Carmona dons another face, fills with familiar noises, lives again. And during these long nocturnal hours, the land of Spain becomes, more than ever, that universe of shadow and light which is so distinctive to the country, and which makes it so captivating.

A bathroom, subtly imbricated into a room by the effect of French windows veiled with curtains.

One of the patios, between the swimming pool and the drawing rooms. Guests enjoy having breakfast here, before the heat of day.

A palm tree offers abundant shade to the pool, which is bordered by antique tiles set in a chevron pattern.

HACIENDA BENAZUZA

~

Centuries of legend reflected in Andalusia

Photos on pages 100, 101, 102 and 103:

Page 100: *Fortified in the fifteenth century by the religious and military order of Santiago, Hacienda Benazuza today shows traces of this past. The hotel uses it as inspiration for its keys and for its logo, symbolizing the ramparts that still dominate the entry porch.*

Page 101: *This patio, with a well, served as the access to the hacienda's main entrance, formerly reserved for the masters. Today it houses the hotel's reception desk (top).*
Details from the chapel's frieze, made of ceramics from the Seville region. Peasants from the surrounding area used to pray at the chapel during Holy Week and Pentecost (bottom, left and right).

Pages 102 and 103: *Bordering the swimming pool, the Alberca, one of the hotel's three restaurants. The hacienda's bronze-colored roofs are reflected in the pool.*

As in every family mansion, horses occupied a central place in the life of the hacienda. Guests notice it as soon as they cross the entry porch, and are almost surprised not to hear the clatter of hooves on the paved ground.

Lost in the Aljarafe, the "high land" near Seville, and baked by the sun where only hundred-year-old olive trees grow, Sanlúcar la Mayor appears at a bend in the road like a large, dazzling white spot. And then you see, set a little apart, Hacienda Benazuza. Proud of its time-honored history, the hacienda dominates the village with its impressive expanse, facing the plane moistened by the languid Guadiamar River. Benazuza is also proud of its new status as a luxury hotel, one of the most refined on the Iberian peninsula.

Centuries of legend coexist here in perfect harmony: the past and the present overlap without ever working against each other. Guests are first aware of the past as they come upon the immense blazon that dominates the fortified porch. Bearing the colors and coat of arms of the Count of Benazuza, the blazonry reminds us that the family's lineage was ennobled as far back as the seventeenth century. Guests notice the hotel's present, too, expressed in the extreme refinement offered by the most modern amenities. Yesterday, as today, the hacienda symbolizes the leisurely pace of life in Andalusia.

In his infinite wisdom, Ferdinand III, better known as Ferdinand the Saint, made no mistake when he distributed the lands reconquered from the invading Moors to his valiant knights. He took care to keep this county, considered the richest and the best situated in Andalusia, for himself. Ever since, Benazuza has lived to the rhythm of Spain's glorious past. Housing for a time the religious and military order of Santiago, the hacienda was fortified in the fifteenth century, which gave the buildings their present

The south gallery, with porticos held up by octagonal columns. Fitted out as private terraces for the hotel's duplex rooms, the terraces offer a peaceful and cool haven for breakfast.

The presidential suite's corbelled loggia. By a trick of the horizontal window panes, you can see, from a perpendicular angle, what is happening below, at your feet.

The swimming pool, designed in the shape of ancient Arab irrigation basins, blends agreeably with the garden.

massive aspect. One hundred years later, Charles I took back the estate and leased it out in order to obtain the funds necessary for his campaigns in Italy and Turkey. Francisco Duarte, a Portuguese, and a former officer of the Spanish royal armies, became the hacienda's first tenant. Under his influence, the hacienda's architecture took its current form. Duarte, a fervent admirer of the Italian Renaissance style, added features never before seen in the Seville countryside, such as an Italian-style patio and a shade garden. Benazuza lost its austere military character and became a genuine residence instilled with joie de vivre and pleasure.

The War of Succession unfortunately marked the beginning of the hacienda's decline. Caught in the maelstrom of the conflict, the estate was divided and changed hands several times before regaining, in the nineteenth century, its past splendor under the guidance of its new proprietor, Pablo Romero, who was famous throughout Spain for breeding a noble herd of bulls. Proud of acquiring the hacienda, the Romero family set its armorial bearings on even the stained-glass window of the main staircase, where they may still be admired today.

Because of its size and importance in ordering local life, the hacienda has always ruled over the region, and most particularly over the destiny of Sanlúcar la Mayor's inhabitants. As much a working farm as a manor, it was here that the villagers came after the olive harvests, up until the beginning of the twentieth century; olive oil was at one time the region's foremost economic resource. The hotel has kept a trace of this activity: a few basins for washing olives stand in the curve of one patio; over there are some gigantic bowls to hold them; a little farther on, an olive press; and finally, the scale. The tools and instruments used for olive cultivation are carefully preserved and exhibited in the hotel's "museum of olive oil," which adjoins the reception desk.

The local peasants also used to come to the hacienda twice a year, during Holy Week and Pentecost, to pray in its chapel. "Lucido Panegiricor predico en la capella de Benazuza es de 1765" may still be read on the recently restored frontispiece, which bears ceramic friezes from Seville.

In realizing their plan for creating a hotel on a site so rich with history, the

Water, an element so precious in this sun-drenched land, is omnipresent, offering an always appreciable sensation of freshness.

A succession of passageways, constructed through the hacienda's ancient outer walls, testifies to the hotel's Moorish past. Passing through, you reach a series of gardens, astonishingly luxuriant under the Andalusian sun.

Elejabeitia family—Benazuza's new owners who come from Bilbao—undertook a crazy mission. The former owners, the Romeros, had ultimately neglected the hacienda, and half of its buildings had even burned down in a fire. Lacking experience in creating and managing a hotel, the Elejabeitias nevertheless did not hesitate to commission a young architect, who was himself a novice in hotel matters. Their trust in the architect was well rewarded.

Javier de Bettencourt, who hails from Seville despite his French-sounding name, began by researching the old construction plans, materials, and colors that at one time were responsible for the splendor of this site. His job turned out to be one of innovation as well as restoration. For instance, the hacienda's buildings and outbuildings had to be enlarged in order to house the number of rooms necessary for the luxury hotel. And thanks to his archival work, Bettencourt rediscovered the exact ocher and orangy beige tonalities of the "noble" patio.

As in every hacienda in Spain, the patio, which provides shade and light as well as a source of coolness, is the focus of the house, around which all of the other rooms are arranged. From the patio, the main staircase in the hacienda leads to the upper-floor rooms which at one time were only occupied in winter. Its sumptuous Mudejar ceiling, decorated with caissons and interlaced wood roses, was re-created

By a subtle effect of halls, leaf doors, and wrought-iron gates, you reach a succession of patios that create oases of freshness throughout the hacienda.

The original ocher and orangy beige colors of the "noble" patio were restored, thanks to the archival research which preceded the hacienda's renovation.

from a fragment of the original design found accidently in one of the rooms.

The Elejabeitias took another chance by giving Manuel Gavira, a young decorator, carte blanche to turn each room into a unique creation, utilizing a variety of colors, fabrics, and furniture. An astonishing blend was born: Gavira mixed Andalusian chairs, Italian headboards, rococo painted ceilings, English curtains and fabrics, baroque canopy beds, Moroccan rugs, and a rustic decor for the bathrooms, without letting any lapse in taste tarnish the blend of genres and periods. From the grand presidential suite, measuring five meters in height; to the intimacy of the hotel's only single room, tapestried in toile de Jouy; each room radiates a sense of well-being due to Gavira's choice of warm colors and noble materials.

The hotel's more uniform public rooms are devoted mainly to the cult of horses, as in the salon-bar, where Andalusian harnesses hang on the walls and richly embellished saddles are set on display. There are even some curious armchairs, upholstered in leather, that you have to straddle in order to sit down.

You can wander casually through the hacienda's succession of small patios, achieved by a subtle effect of hallways, nail-studded leaf doors, and wrought-iron gates, resulting in a series of cool oases. Because the sun's rays can be quite fierce during the day, thick, woven straw mats are lowered on all the windows as was the practice in days gone by.

Andalusia, under Moorish domination

Bulls and horses: Benazuza pays homage to the noble animals of Andalusia

From the floor tiles to the ancient beams of the mezzanine, everything in the bar has been preserved in the original style. Only the bottles are contemporary . . .

The presidential suite: despite its height of five meters, its massive Andalusian furniture, and its impressive fireplace, the suite nonetheless offers warmth and well-being, a result of the mellow colors and noble materials used in its decor.

The salon-bar, devoted entirely to the cult of horses, displays an Andalusian harness, ancient saddles, and even special chairs which you must straddle to sit upon.

The hotel's only single room is completely tapestried in toile de Jouy, which perfectly accentuates the room's intimacy (right).

A painted headboard, inspired by Nicolas Luca de Tena. The motif is different in each room (below, left).

A bathtub with a canopy, improvised to blend with the rustic aspect of the bathroom, which is adorned with marble and ocher-red stucco walls (below, right).

"Nous lirons dans le même lit
Au livre de ton corps lui-même."
Apollinaire

for centuries, has kept some handsome traces of its past. The Arab influence manifests itself in the gardens and terraces, which you reach by passing through the porches of the hacienda's ancient outer wall. Astonishingly luxuriant under the intense heat of the Andalusian sun, each of the gardens has been put to use: in one, herbs—mint, thyme, rosemary, basil—are grown; in another, the scent of magnolia blossoms vies with that of honeysuckle, which itself gets lost amid the fragrances of forty other varieties of flowers; and in yet another, olive trees spread their protective branches over box-tree shrubs. Water, which is precious here, is carefully collected in a series of waterfalls, channels, and fountain basins which by sight alone offer a sensation of coolness. And sitting on the hacienda's terrace amid these gardens at sunset, you can watch the shadows lengthen on the surrounding hills and savor every smell as the land, satiated with heat, slowly begins to exhale the fragrances of a night so long awaited.

The particularly daring decoration in this room is especially attractive to the hotel's Italian and Arab guests. The room features a ceiling painted in the rococo style, showy furniture, and completely gilded headboards.

DROMOLAND CASTLE

~

. . . men might rear in stone
The sweetness that all longed for night and day.

William Butler Yeats

Photos on pages 114 and 115:

Page 114: The O'Brien clan, who founded Dromoland Castle in the sixteenth century, were direct descendants of Brian Boru, the first king of Ireland. The O'Brien coat of arms attests to this royal past.

Page 115: Built in a natural cove, the castle's impressive expanse stands at a bend in the road, hidden from prying eyes but not from the wind, coming up from the nearby sea (top).
View of the lake in front of the castle. The rush, at the edge of the lake, bend but do not break, facing a sea wind that blows without stopping (bottom, left).
The castle's new entrance, set up when Dromoland Castle became a hotel. The entrance is dominated by the blazon of the O'Brien clan who sold the property in the early 1960s (bottom, right).

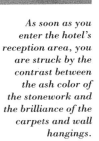

As soon as you enter the hotel's reception area, you are struck by the contrast between the ash color of the stonework and the brilliance of the carpets and wall hangings.

The carved wood panels, running along the walls, add an indispensable touch of warmth to the hotel's public rooms.

The Gothic-style windows were inspired by Thomas Burgh, who advised Sir Edward O'Brien during the castle's construction. Burgh was also the architect for the famous library at Trinity College in Dublin.

After crossing the park gates, you discover, at the end of the road, the impressive façade of Dromoland Castle, located between Limerick and Ennis in western Ireland. A curious confrontation with nature, the castle offers a surprising visual spectacle, where the façade's stonework gets erased, bit by bit, by the orangy brown foam borne by the wind that comes up from the sea a few yards away. For here, the sea breeze blows without letup, making the surface of the lake curl, the rush bend, the oaks crack, as if the elements could break loose at any moment.

As much peaceful harbor as refuge, Dromoland Castle offers immediate comfort to guests who have just come in from braving the outside. The castle's thick walls, carved wood paneling, heavy tapestries, and thick carpets create a protective and reassuring cocoon. And the comforting smell of a wood fire, is permanently maintained by huge logs crackling in the monumental fireplaces. The patina of centuries adds to this sense of well-being. Illustrious ancestors, observing guests debonairly, attest to the castle's past; their portraits fixed for eternity by renowned painters.

For nearly three centuries, the castle's tower has dominated the countryside. Dromoland was built by Sir Edward O'Brien, Baron of Inchiquin, a cousin of the royal family and the proprietor at that time of a good part of western Ireland. He drew up the plans for the castle himself, aided by Thomas Burgh who had recently completed the library at Trinity College in Dublin. Sir Edward also supervised the layout for the castle's vast park, respecting the harmony of its site, a cirque

"La table est le seul endroit où l'on ne s'ennuie jamais pendant la première heure."
Brillat-Savarin

Fine dining has a place of honor at Dromoland Castle. The hotel's French chef was recently distinguished for preparing the best table in Ireland.

*Amid great chambers and long galleries, lined
With famous portraits of our ancestors;*
William Butler Yeats

Gold and gilded details, vestiges of the castle's past, were restored during the renovation undertaken in 1986. The work was directed by Carleton Varney, who also renovated the White House in Washington, D.C.

Photo on pages 120 and 121:
The gallery leading to the hotel's main staircase displays the most important portrait collection in Ireland, almost all devoted to the O'Brien clan.

formed in the mists of time, which may still be admired today. Nature is bountiful in this water-drenched land. Visitors frequently cross doe, hares, and other animals that bring a wild touch to this very well tended park. The site is also home to a golf course, to satisfy players of this Irish national sport.

In the early sixties, Sir Edward's descendants were forced to sell. The castle's purchaser was Bernard McDonough, an American millionaire who had the idea of converting the castle into a luxury hotel. Dromoland Castle became part of the select and coveted circle of country palaces, only possible when mansions of old are turned into hotels. Twenty-five years later, under the control of a consortium of American financiers, the castle underwent a true renewal.

The restoration work is worthy of admiration. Whether in the main gallery, covered with purple hangings, in the drawing room with its pastel tones, or in the dining room hung with crystal chandeliers, gold shines everywhere, the vestiges of Dromoland's past splendors. Other elements—a carved chimneypiece, rounded wood paneling, the ogive of a Gothic window—also recall the rustic castle, as it was conceived by Sir Edward: a dwelling fit for a king, certainly, but also a country house suited to more human dimensions. This perfect marriage is brought to light in every room, combining space, modern comfort, period furniture, and that touch of simplicity which the Irish dispense so easily. And by this union, Dromoland Castle achieves a refined harmony, blending the charms of the past with contemporary comforts.

The drawing room where music recitals were h during the O'Brien era. Today, guests come h to indulge in the pleasures of five o'clock te

Palacio de Seteais

~

*An enchanted palace suspended between
the sea and the mountains of Cintra*

The royal castle of Pena, with its gilded cupolas, still presides over the hills.

Cintra and its hills, as depicted in the antique engravings that decorate the palace's corridors.

Fountains and basins are part of the landscape. The sound of streaming waters and chirping birds blend in the park.

Palacio de Seteais occupies front stage on the mountains of Cintra, in west Portugal. Rising up on a terrace, its standpoint never ceases to seduce visitors. In the nineteenth century, Eça de Queiros, a diplomat and writer considered to be Portugal's greatest novelist, described the site in *The Maias:* "The great plain . . . was strewn with small light green squares and with other darker ones that made [one] think of a sheet all patched together. Small white strips of road meandered between these blotches of color and in the distance, the dazzling whiteness of a village stood out from the hollow of a wood. At every turn, on this land where water abounded, a row of tiny elms revealed the fresh and glistening run of a stream through the grasses. The sea was further out, one smooth line, blurred by a bluish mist over which curved an immense blue sky sparkling like a beautiful enamel, though a trail of mist had stayed there, high up, as if forgotten, and had fallen asleep, all rolled up, suspended in the light. . . ." Only a brisk Atlantic wind sweeping over the land could chase these trails of mist, or with light touches ruffle this landscape, which has lain unchanged over the course of time.

Today we can still understand how Daniel Gildemeester, Dutch by birth and consul for the Netherlands by profession, fell in love with this site when he discovered it almost two centuries ago. A lover of Portugal, Gildemeester was anxious to live out his old age in his adopted country, and this land symbolized for him what was most beautiful about the countryside: a slope of green vales descending in gradual, undulating terraces, giving way to the sea.

Photos on pages 122 and 123:

Page 122: *An alley of oleanders reclaimed from the park's luxuriant growth. In the garden at Palacio de Seteais, man must constantly struggle with nature.*

Page 123: *View of the palace from Campo de Seteais. The design of the building's two wings, joined by a triumphal arch, remains a paragon of architectural classicism (top).*
Passing under the triumphal arch, you reach the terrace; from there, the vista stretches across the countryside to the sea (bottom).

According to legend, the name Seteais came from the cry "ais" (the Portuguese sound for ouch), called out by the common people and repeated seven times by an echo.

The principal entrance to the palace is paved. Elsewhere the flooring is parquet, as here, giving the room a special brilliance in which all the outer splendor is reflected.

Photo on pages 126 and 127:

Detail of the Salon Pillement, named after the French artist Jean-Baptiste Pillement who painted its walls. His style had a considerable influence on Portuguese painting in the eighteenth century.

The echoes of magnificent balls still haunt the salons of Seteais

The backs of three wooden chairs, painted by hand in the Portuguese tradition.

The honorable consul decided to build his country home on this impregnable terrace and then retire there. Some years earlier, in 1755, Lisbon was destroyed by a violent earthquake which some had believed was the end of the world. Afterwards, a frenzy of construction followed, the reaction of many when they want to conquer fear and brave the elements. Cintra, also affected by the earthquake, had to be brought up from the ruins as well. From his terrace, Daniel Gildemeester decided to set an example—and do it handsomely.

He erected a building on the Quinta da Alegria, the domain of joy. At that time, construction was limited to the west wing of Seteais' present-day park. All angles and counterangles, the building radiates power and serenity, mirroring the image of the merchant bourgeoisie. Gildemeester belonged to this class and was among its most illustrious representatives in the Portuguese kingdom. The façade's perfect classicism, which excited the admiration of the age, has permitted the palace to cross the centuries without taking on a single wrinkle. The western part of the building is the same today as it was on that hot night at the end of July 1787, when the high society crowded the palace for its inauguration. Marveling at what he experienced, one privileged witness to these splendors, William Beckford, described the evening: "The illumination was brilliant, [there was] much silver, an enormous table, all the dishes possible to imagine, and a 'flan monté' about fifty or sixty feet long, sparkling from the smooth design patterns and from the silver vases of the best manufacture."

The interior architecture, unchanged to this day, was conceived to welcome such festivities. The main staircase issues onto the gallery whose size and length were calculated to accommodate the grandiose buffets, which at the time did credit to wealthy households. Afterwards, the invited guests could amuse themselves in the various salons, and admire the frescoes and trompe l'oeil decor which remain in excellent condition. Neptune on his chariot still lords over the stately drawing room that occupies one wing of the building. A little farther on, you will find exotic landscapes adorned with chinoiseries by the French artist Jean-Baptiste Pillement, who enjoyed painting in this style and whose work greatly influenced Portuguese painting in the eighteenth century. All that is missing is the rustle of crinolines on the parquet and the laugh of some bedazzled young ladies to complete the illusion and make you feel part of the festivities.

One of the palace's former dining rooms, decorated as in its period of splendor. Today it serves as a reading room.

The bar, opened when Palacio de Seteais became a hotel, is perfectly integrated into the palace, thanks to murals similar to those found in the palace's older rooms.

Detail of the original fresco adorning the principal wall of the main drawing room. A blend of classicism and romanticism, this genre of painting was very fashionable in the eighteenth century.

A bouquet of hydrangeas, the queen flower of the palace gardens, crowns one of the pedestal tables in the main drawing room.

After Gildemeester's death, the palace took on its current dimensions: two wings linked by a triumphal arch in the neoclassical style. The new owner, the king's grand equerry, Marquis de Marialva, undertook this construction in 1797 in order to complement the symmetry of the original building with a second, identical structure. After the embellishment, the Quinta da Alegria was henceforth called Palacio de Seteais, named after the large enclosed field that faces it, through which guests must pass to reach the palace today.

As with every site laden with history, the palace has a legend. For some, the name originated from slurring two words—sete ais, pronounced "set ai." In Portuguese, sete means seven and ais is the cry for ouch. As the legend goes, the cry was called out by the common people on the esplanade. The echo, according to custom, then repeated the cry "ai" seven times. For others, the name Seteais comes from the plural for seto, which in old Portuguese designated a hedgerow, or an enclosed forest full of game.

The ascendancy of nature here makes this second version appear more likely, if less marvelous. There is no doubt that the vast estate owes its name to its environment, proof of the endless battle between man and nature: on one side, a complete domestication symbolized, perhaps to an extreme, by the perfectly straight French-style garden where you can appreciate a panorama that reaches as far away as the foaming sea; and on the other, alleys shaded by oleanders

A painted and gilded wood console, in one of the palace's numerous drawing rooms.

Chandeliers and period carpets in the main drawing room. The large bay windows open onto the terrace, from where you can admire a panorama which extends to the sea.

No anachronisms in this room: to respect the harmony and style of the period, television and minibar were banned.

The banquet gallery, once the site of immense buffets, was where the Portuguese high society came to feast.

entwined by bracken and other climbing plants. The garden offers a surprising mix, with impressive clumps of hydrangeas, tamed, pruned, and embellished by the hand of man, growing next to wilder camellias and box trees. In this garden, which is landscaped in various shades of green, a delightful scent surprises you at every turn, a small stone bench invites contemplation, streaming water echos the chirp of a bird. In every nook and cranny you will discover some fountain, some rare tree variety, some hundred-year-old cedar. As Eça de Queiros wrote, looking out on the park, "In the foreground stood the esplanade, deserted and green, dotted everywhere by yellow buds. At the far end, a thick row of old trees, their trunks covered over with ivy, created a high wall of shining foliage along the gate, and emerging abruptly from this bushy line of sunlit wood, in the full splendor of day, standing out vigorously in a sharp line against the background of clear blue sky, rose the elegant summit of a mountain, all somber violet."

At the end of the nineteenth century,

after a succession of difficult inheritances, the estate fell into disuse. Half a century later, the Portuguese government decided to manage the property and gave Palacio de Seteias a second life, thus creating the most beautiful jewel in Portugal's crown of hotels. Modernized to offer guests the best of today's comforts, the palace has nevertheless kept its soul intact. While every room offers the height of luxury, care was taken to avoid anachronisms (such as minibars, for example), which would not significantly add to the guests' well-being. In the common areas, rearranged during the palace's restoration, the period style was respected, especially in the bar where the murals recall those in the palace's older rooms. Using the landscape and the surrounding gardens like a vast theater, each window has been adorned with heavy curtains, looking as if they are waiting to be closed on the scene they frame, though we will never tire of it. The flamboyant chandeliers and the period furniture and paintings evoke the splendors of yesteryear, and the immense handmade Arraiolos carpets are as magnificent as the carpets once trod upon by the nobility and even by the king, who honored the palace with his presence. The royal castle of Pena still stands on its peak with its shining gold cupolas, dominating the site as befits a lord, watching over the estate, which the ravages of time and the wisdom of men knew to spare—to our everlasting delight.

A Cintra tradition: small pieces of grilled bread served with each meal in the palace's restaurant.

LLANGOED HALL

~

Sir Bernard Ashley's revival of an
Edwardian country house in Wales

In the hall. The romantic portrait of George Henry's wife above the nineteenth-century pianoforte reflects the influence of Japanese painting. Beside the piano, the marble diva seems irritated by the pianist's absence . . .

Two turn-of-the-century ladies wait for gentlemen to come sit and flirt with them.

Photos on pages 136, 137, 138 and 139:

Page 136: *A gate with elegant arabesques, an invitation to discover the park.*

Page 137: *View of Llangoed Hall, park side: the long façade of gray granite, set with mullion windows, looks out at the meadows along the river* (top).
A traditional sight in the Welsh countryside: grazing sheep in a meadow enclosed by low drystone walls (bottom).

Pages 138 and 139: *A bright fairyland: Llangoed Hall's façade from the main courtyard.*

Throughout Europe and particularly in Great Britain, the end of the nineteenth century and the first years of the twentieth century were the golden age of country houses, the large, landed estates where owners lived well and entertained heartily, surrounded by a multitude of faithful and zealous servants like the irresistible P. G. Wodehouse's "inimitable Jeeves." World War I gave the final blow to this prosperous era, synonymous with a way of life that was mirrored in literature, where it was described in either a flattering or an ironic manner.

To glimpse the highly civilized, delightfully Edenic surroundings of British aristocrats as they spent their summer and fall seasons at these country estates, you need only open the novels of Henry James, Thomas Hardy, Anthony Trollope, Vita Sackville-West, E. M. Forster, Virginia Woolf, Edith Wharton, or Evelyn Waugh. Recently, movies have taken over from novelists in depicting this world, often casting a fascinated, nostalgic, as well as critical eye on the customs and lifestyles of this small, select society, as protected from "the sound and the fury" of history as from the mundane problems of existence. From *The Go-between* to *Howard's End*, including such films as *Lady Chatterley's Lover* and *Tess of the D'Urbervilles*, many movies have featured English castles and manors, peopled with complacent, hypocritical gentlemen, avid hunters and heavy drinkers, eccentric old bachelors and ethereal ladies, who were corseted by prejudices and weighed down by class consciousness if they weren't outrageously liberated.

When he purchased Llangoed Hall in 1987, Sir Bernard Ashley yielded, as he readily admits, to a vague nostalgia for this lifestyle that had peaked at the end of the Victorian era. "One of my dearest wishes," he confides, "has always been to find a country hotel that would successfully revive the atmosphere of an Edwardian family reunion. The guests would arrive, tired

The majestic stairwell, in red and black tonalities, illustrates the splendors of Edwardian England.

Today the manor's ancient seventeenth-century door leads into the billiard room.

View of an elegant statue.

Clover or fleur-de-lis? Even the window handles are flowered.

from their trip and weary of their workaday world, to be received warmly and pampered as if they were invited guests, and not simply travelers passing through, here only to occupy a room and fill up the restaurant. Ever since I first saw Llangoed Hall, I was convinced that I could realize my dream of a perfect hotel with[in] this elegant building, and restore it to what it was in the past, a magnificent Edwardian country house."

As is fitting, the passage to paradise is not an easy one. To reach Llangoed Hall, you must travel to Wales—a journey which is in no way heroic, but which seems to frighten some residents of the British Isles—and lose yourself a little in its green hinterland where the villages unfurl names rich with consonants and formidable to pronounce. An hour's drive by car from Cardiff, Llangoed Hall stands in a five-hectare park between a forest and a river. On the horizon, the dark line of the "Black Mountain," covered with snow in winter, pleasantly completes the landscape.

A dwelling is said to have occupied this site since the early Middle Ages. Legend has it that the first Welsh parliament was even held here. According to a more reliable source, a manor in the style of James I was built on this site in 1632 by Sir Henry Williams. His armorial bearings may still be seen above the door in the south wing and over the fireplace in the main drawing room. The Williams family kept the house for almost two centuries, until the years 1810–1820, when the owner at that time had the misfortune to lose Llangoed Hall at cards! The lucky winner did not hold on to his gain for long, however, and the property changed hands several times until the early 1900s.

A solitary tree watches over the house.

Portrait of Colonel John Bowles in the first-floor gallery. The work, by the American painter Hermann Dudley Murphy, surveys visitors with a critical eye.

HERMAN DUDLEY MURPHY

A corner of the music room. From the depths of the comfortable easy chairs next to the piano, you can admire the pine and Irish yew trees in the park. Designed by Laura Ashley, the floral pattern on the curtains and valances echo the flower beds in the garden.

Mrs. Archibald Christy, the wife of a major London hatter, bought the estate and asked the Welsh architect Clough William-Ellis to restore and redesign it. Llangoed Hall was his first important commission. A decade later, he would design the curious project of Portmeirion. Between 1912 and 1919, Sir Clough William-Ellis, as eager as his colleague Sir Edwin Luytens to renew the spirit of old English country houses, enlarged and considerably modernized the house, while preserving the broad outlines of the original manor. Built in local freestone, endowed with large mullion windows, the manor had a slate roof that was so heavy it had to be shored up with small iron beams. The building's most striking features include the ancient library paneled in oak, the dining room, and the majestic wood-carved staircase leading to a long, columned gallery, which in turn leads to the main bedrooms.

Over the course of the century, Llangoed Hall slowly deteriorated, and in the early 1970s it tottered on the brink of ruin, so much so that, despite its historic and architectural interest, it was scheduled to be torn down. The garden surrounding the house had become fallow, and only a visionary like Sir Bernard Ashley could have had an inkling of the

profit to be drawn from this abandoned estate. Three years of intensive work were necessary to restore Llangoed Hall's past splendor and furnish it with every modern amenity. A wing was added to house some new rooms, but the "graft" took so well that the new part is hard to distinguish from the old. Today the hotel offers twenty-three rooms, four of them suites.

From the wallpaper to the fabrics, from the friezes to the curtains, every decorative element presents the gamut of Laura Ashley's design collection. Well-chosen furnishings permit guests to do more than sleep in their rooms: for a bite or an aperitif, they are presented a fruit basket, a carafe of sherry, and a box of biscuits on a coffee table; to relax, there are a pair of comfortable armchairs; to work, a proper desk; and in case of insomnia, they can find some classic old novel by Sir Henry Rider Haggard or by Sir Arthur Conan Doyle on the bookshelves. As was customary in great country houses, many of the beds have testers or four posters. Adjoining the rooms, the bathrooms are not dark little holes but spacious, cheerful rooms in which you can contemplate—from your tub—the rural panorama outside your window. Embedded in paneling lacquered in light colors, the bathtubs and washstands, lined with soaps and bath products from the best perfumeries in London, are in keeping with the manor's impressive and generous spirit.

To get to the ground floor, guests must pass through the long, first-floor gallery that leads from the main bedrooms. It also serves as an art gallery, exhibiting some of the most beautiful paintings in Sir Bernard's private collection. Near the

The dining room, all in a sunny yellow, set for dinner. The English drawings on the walls are from Sir Bernard Ashley's private collection.

The discreetly opulent grand salon, with its immense couches, mahogany desks with caissons, monumental fireplace, and indirect lighting, is as convivial as any guest might wish.

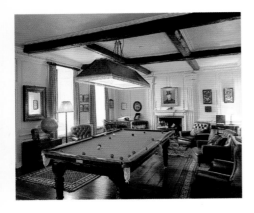

middle of the gallery hangs a work done in the Whistler style; the long-limbed silhouette of Colonel John Bowles who, as portrayed in the painting, seems to be reviewing Llangoed Hall's visitors with an inquisitorial air. The ground floor has a layout similar to the first floor. A large gallery leads to the main courtyard on one side and to the manor's drawing rooms, library, and dining room on the other.

Surprisingly, once you cross Llangoed Hall's threshhold, there is nothing to indicate that this splendid country house is also a hotel: there is no reception desk, no porter, no concierge demanding your passport or your credit card; only a person who asks if you had a good stay and who helps carry your bags.

This impression of being a guest invited into a private mansion is felt even more in Llangoed Hall's vast but welcoming drawing rooms. Centered around an immense stone fireplace, the main drawing room features large French windows opening onto a terrace that overhangs the garden. A Regency table on either side of the fireplace displays a striking collection of liquor bottles from around the world, while a sofa invites you to relax. Opposite, two giant couches could seat an entire rugby team.

A look into one of the rooms. From the wallpaper to the fabrics and friezes, Llangoed Hall reveals the immense variety of Laura Ashley's designs. Among the details that contribute to the guests' well-being: fresh flowers and a carafe of sherry on the table.

*"Les objets neufs te déplaisent ; à toi aussi,
ils font peur avec leur hardiesse criarde,
et tu te sentirais le besoin de les user."*
Mallarmé

"Souffrez que ma fatigue, à vos pieds reposée rêve des chers instants qui la délasseront."
Verlaine

Variations on the art of drapery. The canopy on the left does not indicate the pomp of a king's dais, but the promise of a serene sleep.

Conversation areas are arranged around a coffee or a pedestal table and large, deep armchairs covered in striped fabrics or damasks in warm colors occupy the rest of the salon. Next door the music room, decorated in the floral chintz so characteristic of British country houses, prompts you, if you suddenly feel the desire, to sit down at the piano and improvise. Or if you prefer, after coming back from a walk along the Wye, one of the most beautiful salmon rivers in the country, you may partake in a tea so refined and copious it would have gratified Jane Austen's heroines. The library is a few steps away in the south wing. This room, perhaps the most intimate and convivial room at Llangoed Hall, has two facing fireplaces. Above one hangs a portrait of an Edwardian gentleman in top hat who seems to patronize the library, which is furnished with easy chairs and devoted to male hobbies: billiards, card games, collections of regimental insignia, model ships and trains, back copies of *National Geographic* . . .

This luxury hotel, free of all ostentation, will give you the exquisite sensation of being elsewhere than in a hotel, as if you were visiting exceedingly courteous, hospitable, and relaxed hosts who have the gift of perfect taste. Sir Bernard Ashley has fulfilled the stakes he set for himself, and has re-created the atmosphere of a country house at the time of Edward VII, beyond anyone's wildest hopes.

Opening onto a landscape, the view from the large bay window disappears into the hills of the peaceful Welsh countryside.

Schlosshotel Kronberg

~

The pledge of allegiance of an English princess
who became the empress of Prussia

DIESES HAUS ERBAUTE
IN DEN JAHREN 1889 BIS 1893

VICTORIA

DEUTSCHE KAISERIN UND KÖNIGIN VON PREUSSEN
PRINCESS ROYAL VON GROSSBRITANNIEN UND IRLAND
GEBOREN ZU LONDON AM 21. NOVEMBER 1840
GESTORBEN HIER AM 5. AUGUST 1901

The park's layout and choice of trees were supervised by Empress Victoria, who drew most of her inspiration from English country gardens. Today, the twenty-hectare park she helped landscape has been converted into a golf course.

Photos on pages 150 and 151:

Page 150: *Carved wood martyr adorning the door of the Red Salon. Empress Victoria, who had the castle built at the end of the nineteenth century, personally supervised the furnishing of the interior, down to the slightest details.*

Page 151: *View of the castle from the park. The castle looks the same today as it did one hundred years ago; everything has been preserved despite the decline of the imperial family and Germany's two world wars* (top). *The timber-framing, inspired by both Anglo-Norman and German construction, reflects the architectural compromises found throughout the castle, and reveals Empress Victoria's British origins as well as the demands placed on her as the leading lady of Prussia* (bottom, left).
The commemorative plaque at the hotel's entrance notes that the castle was built between 1889 and 1893 by Empress Victoria, who died here in 1901 (bottom, right).

"No one element should draw attention, but every element must hold it." This was the wish expressed by Empress Victoria—empress of Prussia and widow of Friedrich III, whose reign lasted just barely three months. After his death in 1888, Empress Victoria decided to retire to this parcel of land in the heart of the Taunus forest, several kilometers from Frankfurt, and build a castle where she intended to live out the rest of her life. The empress engaged the renowned Berlin architect Ernst Eberhard von Ihne, and advised him to study the layout of English country houses for inspiration. She insisted on this return to basics—and to her British roots.

The oldest daughter of Queen Victoria, after whom she was named according to tradition, she had left her native country at the age of seventeen to marry Friedrich, prince, consort, and heir to the Prussian kingdom. Her origins had always made her a little suspect to her fellow Prussian citizens, particularly Bismarck, who was too imbued by German nationalism to trust a princess of British blood. But Victoria was able to prove her loyalty to her adopted country by giving six children to the Prussian crown, one of whom became the celebrated Kaiser Wilhelm II.

Victoria was only forty-seven when

The rose garden, with fountain basins, statues, and cypresses is the only element of Italian inspiration at Schlosshotel Kronberg.

she found herself a widow. To prove her loyalty to those who still doubted her attachment to Prussia, she decided to retire to this property outside of Frankfurt and build a castle devoted entirely to the memory of her late husband. Schloss Friedrichshof—it was named Kronberg only in 1953, after it was converted into a hotel—offers a curious architectural compromise between German Gothic and Renaissance English, using the best designs from the Tudor period, specifically those from the Elizabethan era.

Begun in 1889, the castle's construction lasted four years. Local materials were used for the exterior: quartzite extracted from the Taunus mountains for the façade; basalt from the Rhine for the columns; sandstone from Franconia taken from the banks of the Mainz River for the castle's corbeling, windows, and entrance. The empress's influence is felt even more in the interior. The chandeliers and lamps, carved panel doors, wall friezes, stained-glass windows bearing the coat of arms of the imperial family, and fireplaces all reveal a distinctly un-German taste. This is even more striking in the Venetian-style library, located on the ground floor near the hotel's reception desk. The favorite room of Empress Victoria, a woman of great culture, the library was designed for study and meditation, from the frescoes that decorate the mantelpiece to the icons that adorn the wall facings.

Victoria moved into Schloss Friedrichshof in 1893. During the eight years she lived there, she furnished the large castle with the souvenirs and objets d'art she had personally collected with

Empress Victoria retired to this castle after the death of her husband, Emperor Friedrich III. The Royal Suite was the kaiser's favorite room when he came to visit his mother.

The Blue Salon, also called Salon Louis XVI for its furnishings, today serves as a banquet dining room.

The main staircase with the imperial blazon embroidered by the firm of Gobelins.

The entrance to the Venetian library, the favorite room of Empress Victoria.

The entry hall, with its impressive Renaissance-style fireplace, offers the first glimpse of the interior's majesty.

The bronzes collected by the empress are on display in every room and along the hotel's corridors.

A portrait of Emperor Friedrich III in military uniform crowns the Green Salon, today fitted out as a reception hall.

The gilded chambranle and massive door leading to the castle's dining room. Decorated by the empress, the dining room is now the hotel's restaurant.

her husband. Glasses from Venice, porcelain from Limoges, majolica and faience, ivory and bronzes, jewels and watches, all have been preserved; visitors may admire them in the showcases in the main hall, and guests who stay at the hotel may even find some of these period collectibles in their rooms.

Despite the years and two world wars, Schloss Friedrichshof appears today exactly the way Empress Victoria planned it. It has remained the property of the family of Landgraf von Hessen, heirs to the imperial crown. But the castle's size, and especially the immense park surrounding it, became too costly to maintain, so in 1953 the family decided to convert it into a hotel. Renamed Schlosshotel Kronberg, the castle has added a new palace hotel to Germany's luxury hotel offerings, magnificently landscaped with a golf course surrounding it. Empress Victoria's presence is keenly felt to this day, however, whether in the Blue Salon where she chose the fabrics, the Red Salon still dominated by the Gobelins tapestry she hung there, the dining room filled with family portraits, the study where she liked to withdraw in order to paint, or even in the private rooms, which display the furniture and curtains she had selected to welcome her friends.

Schlosshotel Kronberg has become the jewel of German hotels—not the least of the posthumous ironies bequeathed by this great British princess who so much wanted to be loved by her people.

"Make yourself at home and I will do the same."

The lions, whether sculpted on the porch pediments or carved into the stair banisters, recall the empress's British ancestry.

A chest of drawers, with marquetry inlaid with mother-of- pearl, in an upstairs hall.

Photo on pages 158 and 159:
*The Delft and Chinese
faiences displayed in this
room belonged to Empress
Victoria's private collection.*

The study, where Empress Victoria withdrew to paint.

*Frieze ceilings,
wainscoting, and
hangings; each room
has its own soul and
radiates an atmosphere
that reflects the British
more than the German
tradition.*

*The blazons of the royal British and Prussian families illuminate the stained-glass
windows of the main staircase.*

PALUMBO

~

"Donnez-moi le Pausilippe et la mer d'Italie."

Gérard de Nerval

As soon as you enter, the hotel's historical emblem evokes the past of Palazzo Confalone.

Set on the dining room buffet, the shimmering crystal promises conviviality.

Elaborate with geometric designs and floral motifs, the antique faience paving adds freshness to the entry hall.

The village of Ravello spreads out like a sunny terrace between sea and mountain, dominating the Gulf of Salerno and the resort towns of Amalfi and Maiori. Founded by Romans in the sixth century, Ravello was for a long time one of the busiest trading centers on the Mediterranean. An architectural testament to these prosperous exchanges with the Orient, Palazzo Confalone was a lord's mansion in the twelfth century, reorganized in the early seventeenth century, and today ranks as an important example of the distinctive composite style, rich in Arab-Oriental influences, that developed on the Amalfi coastline.

The setting for the current Palumbo hotel, the antique Palazzo Confalone has preserved its original medieval structure and atmosphere. The palazzo belongs to the Vuilleumier family, who settled in Ravello in 1875, the year Pasquale Palumbo, having left his native Switzerland, opened the first Palumbo hotel inside the Palazzo Episcopio with his wife Elisabeth Wartburg.

In 1928 the hotel's quarters moved to an adjacent building, Palazzo Sasso. During this period, Pasquale Vuilleumier, the nephew of Pasquale Palumbo, acquired Palazzo Confalone to make it his private residence. Twenty-four years later, this palazzo was also turned into a hotel. In 1978, it had only five rooms and no restaurant. Gradually, other rooms and suites were added: a dining room, bar, hall salons, and then a panoramic restaurant. Today, Pasquale's son, Marco Vuilleumier, receives guests in the hotel's great Moorish hall. An ancient medieval cloister covered by glass, the

Photos on pages 162, 163, 164 and 165:

Page 162: *Interlaced branches cover the pergola, offering cool shade to guests who linger here during the hot hours.*

Page 163: *Overlooking the Gulf of Salerno and its infinite views, the terrace encourages reverie at the dinner hour (top).*
From the arbor, glimpses of lush garden nooks (bottom, left).
The uneven surfaces of the Pompeiian red and Neapolitan yellow façades, standing 350 meters above the sea, reflect the hotel's successive architectural developments (bottom, right).

Pages 164 and 165:
On the vast terrace, pillars laden with greenery frame the hills that descend to the ancient cities of Maiori and Paestum.

An antique capital crowns a column. In the twelfth-century palazzo, traditional styles mix with Oriental influences.

The reception hall's series of arcades, typical of Arab Norman architecture, rest on columns of blonde marble

Moorish hall features a rhythmical series of arcades typical of Arab-Norman architecture, resting on marble columns brought back from the Orient. The hall's majolica paving, in polychrome ceramic with geometric designs and floral motifs, is sumptuously set off by the luminously bare walls.

Palumbo's five floors are linked together, from the garden to the highest rooms, by a sequence of unexpected vaults, passages, alcoves, and recesses. This overlapping effect is due to the architectural and decorative elements added in the seventeenth century, as well as to differences in the heights of the parts added as the hotel was enlarged. The reception hall has a monumental staircase that leads to the loggia and the upper floors. Around the reception hall there are also two salons, a bar as precious as a Moorish jewel, and a terrace. Below a romantic pergola hung with millions of roses, the narrow, balcony-like terrace is where guests like to linger at nightfall, glass in hand, facing the panorama of the bay of Amalfi and listening to the sound of cicadas.

Since it first opened, the Palumbo hotel has welcomed illustrious guests from around the world, drawn not only by the beauty of the site but also by the beauty of Signora Palumbo, née Elisabeth Wartburg. The voluminous guest register, begun in 1875 when the hotel was still only a pension, counts out notable signatures page after page: Henri de Montherlant, Paul Valéry, Princess Nina Galitzine, François Mitterand, Truman Capote, Tennessee Williams, Ingrid Bergman. . . .

There is nothing really astonishing

A warm juxtaposition of elements: a graciously dressed table, an arched alcove in gilded wood, and a masterpiece from the Caravaggio school.

Restaurant view: the panoramic terrace where guests sample the hotel's traditional Mediterranean cuisine, accompanied by a bottle of house "Episcopio" wine.

Another restaurant view: the interior dining room, in the extension of the terrace, offers diners a more subdued retreat.

Detail of a painted panel (left).

All in curves, the Palumbo hotel's exquisite Moorish bar provides an exotic setting (below, left).

An elegant, symmetrical composition of objects set on a chest of drawers (below, right).

about this. Ravello, clinging to the wooded hills of the Lattari mountains that plunge down to the sea, with its winding lanes, antique villas, terraces jutting out over the abyss, fragrant pergolas, and legendary gardens, has remained for more than a hundred years one of the most sought-after and evocative settings in Europe.

Richard Wagner, arriving in 1880, was inspired by the gardens of the Villa Ruffolo to model Klingsor's magic garden after them in Parsifal. D. H. Lawrence stayed here several times between 1926 and 1927 to write *Lady Chatterley's Lover*. And in the spring of 1938, Greta Garbo rented Villa Cimbrone—the palace built at the beginning of the century by an eccentric English lord, William Beckett, now belongs to Pasquale Vuilleumier's brother—to enjoy a secret tryst with the conductor Leopold Stokowsky.

And it was also in Ravello that King Victor Emmanuel III abdicated, on April 12, 1946, in favor of his son Umberto, who later formed the first government of national unity, the basis for the present Italian republic.

In the last decade, numerous musical programs have been organized in Ravello, including a Wagner festival at Villa Ruffolo, as well as a variety of concerts held at the cathedral, the church of San Francesco, and the town's public garden.

"Et toi, Italie, un jour à genoux,
J'ai baisé pieusement la terre tiède, tu le sais."
Valery Larbaud

The rough beauty of a wrought Renaissance coffer, on top of which is arranged a row of majolica plates.

On a balcony, the wrought-iron orangery table's delicate volutes are thrown into relief by the rectilinear bar rails.

the rooms are enhanced by antique furniture, ceramics from Vietri, Greco-Roman columns, rounded glass bays, paintings from the sixteenth and seventeenth centuries, gilded alcoves, and waxed terra-cotta flooring. . . .

When Marco Vuilleumier accompanies us to the entry gate and we notice Palumbo's tactful hotel sign, we cannot help but think that true, unalterable elegance doesn't advertise itself. Charm cannot be flaunted—it has to be offered naturally, with the greatest discretion.

Dining at Palumbo is as renowned as the hotel's splendid site. The restaurant's dining room is located on the first floor near the salons, which are sumptuously decorated with seventeenth-century frescoes. In the restaurant, guests may sample the hotel's famous house "Episcopio," a regional table wine found in most of the restaurants on the bay of Amalfi. With a bit of luck, Marco Vuilleumier might even take you on a tour of the cellars. Below the hotel annex, the wine cellars are fitted out with enormous hundred-year-old wood barrels. There, in the coolness of the crypt, you might taste a glass of white, red, or rosé.

Each of the rooms and suites at the Palumbo hotel has an individual character. Avoiding traditional hotel numbering, the rooms are distinguished by their names: La Romantica, the Persian Suite, the Duke's Room, the Dovecote, and the Tower among them. Displaying an ingenious use of space and a concern for decorative restraint,

Windows and mirror in Romanesque arcades in a bathroom create an effect as mysterious as a chapel.

The chic and restraint of a large, elegantly striped bed is reflected in the Empire swing mirror.

Excelsior Vittoria

~

A terrace hotel above the bay of Sorrento evokes
the grand tour of the nineteenth century

View from the Piazza Tasso: the hotel's belle époque sign crowns an arbor that leads to the seashore (right).

La Vittoria, with its impeccable gardens, trees, and potted flowers capping Roman columns, is the oldest of the three villas that form the hotel complex (below).

Above the Tyrrhenian Sea, Victorian-style tables and chairs on Vittoria's large terrace shaded by two olive trees. An incomparable view of the Bay of Naples and Mount Vesuvius (opposite).

*"Sur la plage sonore où la mer de Sorrente
Déroule ses flots bleus au pied de l'oranger,
Il est, près du sentier, sous la haie odorante
Une pierre petite, étroite, indifférente
Aux pieds distraits de l'étranger…"*

Photos on pages 174, 175, 176 and 177:

Page 174: *For a pleasant lunch or dinner in fresh surroundings, the Stuart dining room offers a setting where the simplicity of the furniture matches the elegance of the room's proportions.*

Page 175: *Overhanging the Bay of Naples, suspended between sea and sky, Excelsior Vittoria's whimsical trio of façades is bordered with large balustrade terraces (top). Detail of the splendid eighteenth century fresco on the wide ceiling of Vittoria's dining room. Garlands, wildflower bouquets, and cherubs are entangled around the trompe l'oeil balustrade hemming the vault (bottom).*

Pages 176 and 177:
Overall view of the majestic restaurant, Vittoria's most impressive room. The waxed parquets reflect the blue and gold splendor of the dining room's painted ceiling.

A stay at the Grand Hotel Excelsior Vittoria of Sorrento revives the bygone era of the grand tour and other aristocratic nineteenth-century holidays, when the cosmopolitan high society, including Goethe, Lord Byron, Oscar Wilde, and Alphonse de Lamartine—who penned these famous verses, came to spend the winter at the foot of Mount Vesuvius.

The arrival at the Excelsior is unforgettable, whether you get there by road, following the long, shady alley of olive, orange, and lemon trees, or you approach by sea, captivated by the vista of balustrade terraces overhanging the Bay of Naples. This experience is unique to the Excelsior, since on one side it offers the proximity of Sorrento and on the other, an incomparable panorama encompassing the Bay of Naples, Mount Vesuvius, as well as the islands of Procida, Ischia, and Capri.

Built into volcanic rock on an archaeological site (in 1948, Roman columns were found in the garden's subsoil), the Excelsior's three buildings,

A delicate gouache in medallion form, used for publicity, immortalizes the port of Sorrento and the Grand Hotel Vittoria as they appeared in 1886.

each of different architectural inspiration but bound by a common destiny, are linked together to form the hotel complex such as we see it today. To the south stands the oldest villa, La Vittoria; to the north, La Rivale, built in 1882; and caught between these two, the unexpected silhouette of a Swiss chalet, La Favorita, built in the 1920s on the whim of a British lord. (Originally, there was also a fourth villa, La Caporiva. Built in 1924 to enlarge the hotel, the Gothic-style building was badly damaged by the earthquake of 1980 and was subsequently demolished.)

The Excelsior has belonged to the Fiorentino family for four generations. Its history began in 1834, the year La Vittoria was built, when the current owner's great-grandmother, a Madama Rispoli, married Raffaelle Fiorentino. At the end of the nineteenth century, the hotel's name changed from Rispoli to Vittoria. The adjective "Excelsior" was added in the 1920s. Another fact worth noting is that the steam motor, which operated the cable railway that brought guests from the port to the hotel in the early part of the century, was also used at

night as an electric generator. (Today, the railway has been replaced by an elevator.) Since 1982, Luca Fiorentino and his wife Lydia have devoted themselves to the restoration and safekeeping of this Victorian setting. First they reopened La Vittoria and La Favorita. Then, in 1984, they opened La Rivale, whose careful repair cost them two years of construction work and some three billion lire.

Lydia Fiorentino took the initiative in rearranging Vittoria's interior. For the decoration, she called on the Belgian artist Thierry Bosquet, the scenographer for Béjart. He put himself in charge of painting the trompe l'oeil frescoes, representing the four seasons, on the main staircase. He also adorned the walls in the Tarantella, the hotel's assembly room, and those in the eccentric Moro Salon. During the restoration, original frescoes painted in the eighteenth century by Luca Fiorentino's great-granduncle were found.

Without modifying the hotel's atmosphere, Luca Fiorentino has magnificently maintained its pure nineteenth-century character, imbued with so many historical presences. But if you ask him to explain the philosophy of

Detail of the wall decoration in Vittoria's dining room. The refinement of the 1930's ceramics meets the less polished sumptuousness of the red marble.

The music room emanates a soothing atmosphere, with potted plants and 1900's furniture created in the Smith-style tradition by Sorrento artisans.

The winter garden, bathed in a sea-green light reflected by the walls and the clear marble flooring. The furniture is from the 1920s (opposite).

The hotel's vast garden planted with olive, orange, and lemon trees, climbing roses, and wildflowers (left).

The entrance to the winter garden. Beyond, the hotel's large alley and the terrace overlooking the sea (bottom, left).

Another view of the winter garden: its brightest section is used for reading. This room, with a frescoed ceiling, is called the Writing Salon (bottom, right).

the hotel, he immediately answers, "A home away from home!" And indeed, despite its impressive history, you do feel at home here, seated in one of the winter garden's wicker chairs enjoying the refined simplicity of a cup of tea, drinking a cocktail in the shade of the dwarf palm trees on the large terrace, hung between sky and sea, or enjoying a moment of meditation in the tranquility of the reading room. Discovering the different rooms in the hotel one after another, you can appreciate the various elements of the lush decor: old posters from the beginning of the century, ceramic tile flooring from Vietri, blue-green monochrome walls, as well as the beauty of the furniture, the profusion of green plants, and the skillfully executed friezes and neobaroque stuccos.

The hotel has 120 rooms, including ten suites. The most famous is the Enrico Caruso Room, which boasts a large terrace that opens onto the port. The famous tenor occupied this room in 1921 before he died in Naples. Overlooking the bay, the rooms feature open-worked voile

*The sober lines of
Stuart Hall's
furniture and the
freshness of its white
and blue ceramic.*

*Detail of an eighteenth-century corner fresco in
the large restaurant dining room. The cherubs
were painted in a trompe l'oeil decor, taking into
account the viewer's perspective.*

*Ceramic decoration created especially for
La Vittoria's exterior façade.*

curtains bought in England, radiators from the 1900s, antique iron beds, delicately shaped dressing tables, and handsome vaults and moldings. As for the fresh-looking bathrooms, each is marbled and displays a different ceramic decor.

Numerous celebrities and prestigious figures have walked through the hotel's wide vestibule, the glass-enclosed winter garden, and the hotel's series of salons with ceilings painted in the Liberty style. At one time, the emperors of Austria-Hungary and the crowned heads of Sweden may have crossed paths with Wagner, Verdi, Alexandre Dumas, or Nietzsche. . . . More recent guests have included Princess Margaret (one of the rooms bears her name), Ronald Reagan, Sophia Loren—who stayed in the Aurora Suite, and Luciano Pavarotti. To get an idea of the hotel's renown, you only need to consult the pages of its guest register.

The Excelsior has two restaurant rooms: the Vittoria dining room, with a waxed parquet, where guests dine pleasantly under the vault of a vast painted ceiling; and the Bosquet terrace, where they may dine facing the purplish mantle of Mount Vesuvius. On the terrace, they can sit right up against the hotel's stone balustrade, decorated with busts from the nineteenth century.

A buffet with dancing is scheduled every week. "The cuisine must please all of my guests. Also, we are interested in revisiting Neapolitan and Italian recipes," emphasizes Luca Fiorentino. In fact, a majority of guests staying at the Excelsior are foreigners, sixty percent of them English. Young people of all nationalities stay at the hotel on their honeymoons, as

"O région du ciel (n'es-tu pas saphir, d'azur et d'argent) Région du ciel enchaînée Au milieu des flots qui se font... Pareils à un autre ciel." Valery Larbaud

Classic marble bust adorning the stone balustrade overhanging the Tyrrhenian Sea.

Breakfast at dawn, sheltered by the arcades of La Vittoria's covered terrace.

Detail of the marble and enamel English taps for the bathtub in the Margaret Suite, named in honor of Princess Margaret who often came to stay at Vittoria (right).

Purified line of the white, wooden balconies above the azure coastline, on the sixth floor of La Rivale (below, left).

The salon of the Margaret Suite displays the mellow, warm tonalities of the ensemble, the refinement of the painted ceiling, and an audacious mixture of styles (below, right).

The bedroom of the Aurora Suite, with the slightly antiquated charm of the ceiling painted in the nineteenth century. Sophia Loren stayed here when she played the role of a cleaning woman in a movie filmed at the hotel in 1984 (opposite).

do businessmen—all drawn by the purely cultural tourism offered by Sorrento.

The hotel has eighty-five employees, including five gardeners who maintain the property. Its five hectares comprise a traditional garden, an orange grove, and olive trees whose olives yield a highly refined oil. There is also a swimming pool, built at the guests' request in 1964; it is on a site that, before the war, was the location for a tennis court, then a soccer field, and finally a large parterre of flowers.

As we leave the hotel, taking again the two-hundred-meter alley that leads back to the center of town, we cannot prevent ourselves from turning around to cast one last look at Vittoria's Pompeiian red and Neapolitan yellow façade. We feel as if we are leaving an oasis of serenity, a spot ranked above all others as much for the magnificence of its site as for the generosity of its owners. The Fiorentinos have achieved their goal: Excelsior Vittoria is not just one more grand hotel, but a welcoming house we feel we have always known.

Photos on pages 186 and 187:

Page 186: *The main staircase serving four floors, each devoted to a different season from fall to summer. Every fresco was created by the contemporary decorator Thierry Bosquet. In the foreground, a statue of Victory sculpted in the nineteenth century.*

Page 187: *The luminous Palace-style bathroom of Room 205, named the Margaret Suite, displays clear marble flooring and sea-green walls.*

Photo on pages 190 and 191:
Breaking with the opulence of Vittoria's large dining room, Stuart Hall is characterized by a more casually elegant atmosphere.

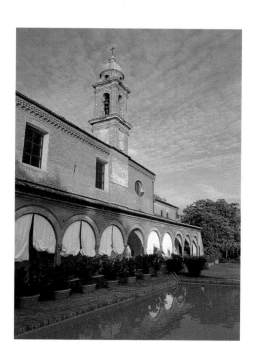

CERTOSA DI MAGGIANO

~

The splendid retreat of a
Carthusian monastery in Tuscany

A corner of the garden planted with olive trees, camellias, and fruit trees. From under a grape-laden pergola, you can gaze out on the bluish hills of the countryside in the distance (right).

Entry portal opening onto the cream-colored cloister. The ogives of the vaulted ceiling rest on slender columns of pietra serena, and the walls still show some traces of the ancient frescoes (below, left).

A monumental door; for us, its closure retains the mystery of the disciples of St. Bruno (below, right).

Photos on pages 192 and 193:

Page 192: *The art of feeling at home at the hotel: Certosa di Maggiano's reading room, set within a library in an eighteenth-century English style, offers deep, comfortable couches, antique leather armchairs, a billiard table, and a generous selection of art books.*

Page 193: *The best angle to view the architectural complex of the monastery, including the fragile campanile, the church's compact building, and the only original wing of the great cloister. Today, the hotel's swimming pool stretches along its wall (top).*
Intersecting ogives in the small entry cloister. Displaying austerity and refinement, the vault symbolizes the spirit of the entire charterhouse (bottom, left).
The Carthusian monks used to collect pure rainwater in this well at the center of the small cloister. The light arch that holds up the cistern repeats, in perfect symmetry, the arcades that border the cortile (bottom, right).

"Nothing on earth can compare with Siena," wrote the great American critic Bernard Berenson, who made Tuscany his adopted home and Italian art the passion of his life. Siena is an incomparable city, as much for its unity of colors as for its proportions. Dubbed the "Pompeii of the Middle Ages" by the nineteenth-century French philosopher and critic Hippolyte Taine, Siena actually dates back to the Etruscans. Afterwards, it became a Roman colony, and today Siena still proudly displays the Roman emblem of the she-wolf and twins.

When you tour Siena, be sure to stop at the marvelous Piazza del Campo. Shaped like a shell of pink bricks, the piazza unfurls an irregular design and a concave surface. Then pause by the Duomo, where you can admire the flourishing vegetation carved into the marble on its façade. Visit, too, the Palazzo Buonsignori, which houses a national art gallery with an impressive collection of Sienese masterpieces.

Certosa di Maggiano is perfectly integrated into this harmonious ensemble. Hidden away in the countryside south of Siena, it is the oldest Carthusian monastery in Tuscany. The certosa (charterhouse) was built in

The reading room, also called the library-smoking room, or, the large game room. In a harmony of red, green, and sepia, the salon is furnished with two couches in a striped fabric designed by Enzo Mongiardino.

The wide strip of Tuscan countryside evokes
the backgrounds of Italian primitive paintings,
deepening the perspective of the meadow.
Outlined against the meadow, the pool and the
beginning of the garden (left).

A Tuscan still life, the earthy flavors of regional
produce and Vin Santo. The charterhouse's
dining room, listed among the best in restaurant
guides to the area, offers such typically Sienese
dishes as rabbit with artichoke hearts
(below, left).

An almost abstract composition: different
varieties of pasta blended into a skein of colors
(below, right).

1316 by order of Cardinal Petroni. Converted into a hotel in 1975, it offers all the services of a grand hotel, a strict respect for the independence of each guest, and the luxury befitting a hotel that has belonged to the prestigious Relais et Châteaux chain since 1976. At the reception desk, the young proprietor, Margherita Grossi, greets the guests with sincere warmth. She attends to her duties briskly but without appearing to bustle about, and when she has time, she joins her guests by the side of the pool to discuss the history and architecture of the monastery, created more than six centuries ago to house the disciples of St. Bruno.

Margherita's relatives, Anna Grossi Recordati and her husband, Adalberto Grossi, an internationally renowned heart surgeon, purchased this unique complex in 1969. At the time, all that remained of the ancient Tuscan charterhouse were superb ruins. During the four years required for the restoration, Anna Grossi Recordati carefully followed each aspect of the work. Above all, it was meant to restore the sober design of this group of buildings which were originally conceived for a contemplative life.

The hotel's fourteen rooms, including

*The wood buffet, painted in trompe l'oeil to imitate
marble, has pride of place in a corner of the dining room.
The buffet is covered with polychrome ceramic dishes
decorated by different artists. On the ceiling, a massive
wrought-iron chandelier with a plant motif.*

nine suites, each have a unique feature, such as a private garden, a roof terrace, or a mezzanine bathroom. All overlook the small inner cloister, the tennis court, or the garden.

To reach the garden, you must walk through a series of rooms: the Salon of Emperors, so named for its seventeenth-century Venetian paintings portraying the emperors of Rome; the reading room, set within a library in an eighteenth-century English style, offering sofas covered in a striped silk fabric created in Florence; and the game room, containing a magnificent alabaster chessboard from Volterra and pages from a nineteenth-century anatomy book framed on the walls. You then enter the winter dining room, one of the most pleasant at the hotel. This room displays painted tables and chairs, as well as a whimsical antique-style buffet which holds up a collection of unique plates designed by different artists.

After passing through these rooms, you enter the only wing that remains of the large cloister. This ancient wing opens onto the hotel's swimming pool and garden. Today, the obelisk that marked the center of the cloister is all that remains.

Margherita Grossi rejoins us as we sit in the garden amid olive trees and camellias. With a lightly cracked voice she tells us about her numerous projects: she plans to organize country festivals to open the monastery even more to the outside world, cover the swimming pool and hold a major classical music concert there, start a literary salon, publish an exhaustive history of the charterhouse. . . . And as we listen, we secretly hope that the Carthusian monastery will remain, for as long as possible, a place of silence.

Variations on a theme: under the vaults of the small cloister, blind arches and discreet niches multiply to infinity the Romanesque figure in the half-circle.

A harmonious marriage of quattrocento art and Tuscan nature. The civilized refinement of the columns is enriched by the contrast with the rough bark of the tree trunks.

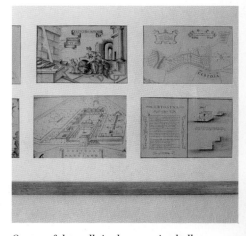

On one of the walls in the reception hall, engravings and ancient layout plans celebrate the history of the oldest Carthusian monastery in Tuscany.

Served in the rooms on an embroidered napkin, the copious breakfast tray is an homage to homemade cooking: the jams, cake, and butter all come from the hotel's kitchen.

The Salon of Emperors honors classical Italy. The salon is named for the seventeenth-century Venetian paintings portraying the emperors of Rome, inlaid in frescoes above the chintz sofas.

TORRE DI BELLOSGUARDO

~

*A garden of Eden
on the hills above Florence*

One of the numerous pianos that furnish the ground-floor salons. The pianos were played by Luigino Franchetti, a renowned pianist and the father of Bellosguardo's current owner (right).

A lofty opening onto the tamed exuberance of Bellosguardo's gardens. The current owner, Amerigo Franchetti, relandscaped the gardens in 1980 (below, left).

Glimpsed through a romantic gap in the greenery, one of the barred windows of the façade adorned with frescoes. Washed out by rain, the frescoes were restored in 1991 (below, right).

Photos on pages 200 and 201:

Page 200: *View seen when arriving on foot from Porta Romana: after taking a path bordered with olive trees, you cross an arbor, then see the entrance to the veranda—a former courtyard for carriages—topped by a loggia.*

Page 201: *View seen when arriving by car: an alley of hundred-year-old cypresses leads to the Renaissance villa. Its buildings are organized around a hunting tower. A statue of Charity sculpted by Francavilla at the end of the sixteenth century stands on the pediment of the entry portal (top).*
Vista from the swimming pool: the city of Florence spreads out below. The sight overwhelmed Dante's friend, Guido Cavalcanti, who named the site "Bellosguardo" (beautiful view) (bottom).

I magine that we are in Tuscany, in the streets of Florence surrounded by ancient palaces with their rugged embossments and their loggias open to the sky. Suddenly, at the end of a piazza, we catch a glimpse of some green hill or bluish peak. An irrestible urge overtakes us to climb up to get a view of the entire city and valley. Driving, we cross the Arno to reach the Porta Romana south of the left bank. The road, lined with historic villas and groves of olive trees, winds through fields until we finally reach the summit of Bellosguardo. After passing through an ancient gate and a long alley bordered with hundred-year-old cypresses, we see a cinquecento façade with a monumental door crowned by a statue, frescoes with geometric motifs, and barred windows. Behind the façade rises a square hunting tower built in the thirteenth century—we have arrived at Torre di Bellosguardo. Before going inside, we continue past it to see the view over Florence. Down some steps to the right we reach the pool, located in a green meadow. The city of Florence spreads out below, silent and languid at our feet, and we feel as if we are touching eternity.

History has it that Guido Cavalcanti, a young Florentine noble, came up to these

The monastic dignity of the hotel's hieratic reception ha
The ceiling and the wall friezes in this spacious ha
which once served as a ballroom, were decorated
Bernardino Poccetti at the end of the sixteenth centur

Photo on pages 204 and 205:
The high arcades of the veranda where guests can enjoy a sunny breakfast in summer. In winter, it becomes an enclosed garden to protect the lemon trees.

In the middle of the former ballroom's ceiling vault, a fresco representing Charity, painted by Bernardino Poccetti in 1580.

A detail of a mural in the music room, imitating an ancient architectural motif.

Eighteenth-century style decorative frescoes painted on plaster in the embrasures of the ballroom windows.

hills for a walk with his friend Dante Alighieri. Enthralled by the panorama of the plain of Florence, Cavalcanti decided to name the hill "Bellosguardo" (beautiful view). On its summit, he built a tower, ordering that the structure, which was about four stories high, have windows opening onto the four cardinal points.

Turning back to the hotel entrance, our field of vision takes in the parklike terraced gardens. Spread over seven hectares, their orderly profusion is laid out in a labyrinth of colorful alleys, perfect lawns, and pergolas sagging under fragrant trails of roses, wisteria, and magnolias. Before entering the spacious palace—built against the hunting tower at the end of the sixteenth century by the Michelozzi family—we cast one last look at the façade. The delicate frescoes on its faded, roughcast surface were restored in 1991, and a statue of Charity by Francavilla dating from 1596 crowns its pediment.

"Silence and serenity are absolutely important," says Amerigo Franchetti. In 1980, he left a brilliant career in advertising to restore Bellosguardo. He tells us about the adventurous history of this site, which appears to stand grandly independent above the city immobilized below. First, he speaks of the tower, confiscated from the Cavalcantis by the Medicis in 1512. The tower belonged to them until 1583 when it became the property of the Michelozzi family, who added various buildings to the solitary belfry. They owned the elegant villa until the beginning of this century. In 1913, it was acquired by Baroness Marion Hornstein, the wife of Baron Giorgio Franchetti, and in 1920 she

. . . escutcheoned doors,
And buildings that a haughtier age designed.
William Butler Yeats

Wrought Renaissance-style wood ceiling in one of the vast rooms on the second floor. The windows overlook Florence and the hotel's garden.

Near the veranda, one of the entry doors to the former ballroom. The blazon of the Michelozzi family is stamped into the pediment.

Under the ceiling vault, a canopied polychrome wood bed. The bed once belonged to the first wife of Luigino Franchetti.

turned Bellosguardo into a kind of guest house where numerous celebrities came to stay. The guest register, which she handled personally until 1948, attests to their visits: drawings, photographs, postcards, poems, concert programs; the signatures of such notables as Prince Erik of Denmark, Lucrezia Corsini, Baron d'Orville. . . .

When the baroness died, the property came to her son Luigino, a renowned pianist. Not knowing what to do with the residence, he rented it to various American colleges for twenty-five years. His son, Amerigo, inherited Bellosguardo in 1978. Two years later, aided by his wife Michelle, Amerigo applied himself to the building's restoration. To save the site and make it profitable, he had to obtain permits to undertake restructural work. The hotel, designed for a public that seeks the atmosphere of a guest house more than the anonymous comfort of a palace hotel, finally opened its doors in April 1988.

A brick-paved veranda, aligned with the vast hall, is converted in winter into an enclosed garden to protect the lemon trees. Around this ancient loggia are salons, a dining room, a small bar, and still more rooms, all with fireplaces in pietra serena, antique furniture, Persian rugs, and pianos. The former ballroom, now a reception salon, is decorated with murals painted by Bernardino Poccetti in 1580.

Upstairs, we find that each room or suite has its own unique cachet: one displays an eighteenth-century caisson ceiling carved with roses; another, a soothing vault; and a third, polychrome window embrasures. A fouth room has a fresco that disappears into an alcove. The beds are all different, too. Some are set on platforms while others have white canopies or rush posters. The tower features a suite that rises on two levels. In another apartment suite, the Gothic windows overgrown with wisteria remind us of the gardens outside.

We leave the shade of the upstairs and return to the gallery on the ground floor. The gallery, directly opposite the entry door, extends a view of arcades laden with greenery. After passing through it, we cross a wild meadow, then a more civilized vegetable garden, before we go down a path, traced out between the olive trees, that ends at the Via Romana. And when we return to the hotel, recrossing the perfect silence of La Torre di Bellosguardo's corridors to gaze on Florence one last time before night completely envelops the city, we feel serene.

In one of the vaulted rooms on the ground floor, an authentic Renaissance bed and elaborate wainscoting partially conceal an ancient mural.

More in the nineteenth-century spirit, this room features three windows and the famous "Cotto" ceramic tiling created in Florence at the end of the last century.

GIDLEIGH PARK

~

A country retreat in the
heart of Cornwall

211

A teak bench for the ritual tea in the garden.

Perennial flower beds at their peak.

Rhododendrons line the river below the terraces.

Dartmoor, a national park spreading out through the heart of Devon in southwest England, is a vast, wild territory. Granite mountains alternate with water-drenched valleys, and large moors covered with heather contrast with green pastures grazed by herds of wild ponies and black-faced sheep. For centuries, Dartmoor remained an agricultural region, mostly devoted to animal husbandry. The roads, hemmed in by high hedges, are so narrow and winding that passing another vehicle is hazardous. Traveling along one of these woodland lanes, as romantic and adventurous as you could wish, you arrive at Gidleigh Park. The manor takes its name from a nearby hamlet, which had been the property of Gydda, the mother of King Harold, in the Middle Ages. Gidleigh Park was built, in pseudo-Tudor style, by an Australian tycoon in the early 1920s. The manor's long white façade is crisscrossed by timber-framing of darkened wood; the brown-tiled roofs feature triangular setbacks sloping forward above spacious bow windows; and the windows themselves have small panes set in lead. Abutting the forest, the manor overhangs a terraced garden and the North Teign River. Rapid and capricious, it flows over a bed of reddish granite rocks, coursing through rhododendron groves. In the distance, the hills of Nattedon and Meldon fence in the horizon with their soft green undulations.

Americans Paul and Kay Henderson, who had no particular hotel experience, purchased the property more than fifteen years ago. Because the estate had been neglected for half a century, they first had to clear out a forest of rhododendrons and

Photos on pages 210 and 211:

Page 210: *The hall clock offers a rhythm to the blissful timelessness of a stay in the country.*

Page 211: *The manor stands at the edge of the forest. Built in 1923 on the foundations of a sixteenth-century building, Gidleigh Park dominates the Teign River valley (top). A deliciously British mixed border (bottom, left). A granite staircase leads from the terrace to the garden (bottom, right).*

Borders of dwarf box trees and santolinas in the formal garden.

A romantic bridge strides over the Teign River.

A dream cottage in which to lead the life of a
Robinson Crusoe, enamored of comfort (left).

*View of the rolling green park through the
bow windows* (below).

azaleas that had returned to the wild in
Devon's damp climate and naturally rich
humus. With the advice of their gardener,
Keith Mansfield, the Hendersons
combined meadows, trees, and river into
a splendid garden of Eden. And they did
it so skillfully that at Gidleigh Park, it is
hard to tell where nature ends and artifice
begins. The aquatic garden, with its water
stairs and its heath ground cover, appears
natural, but was landscaped in the 1980s.
Wildflowers proliferate in the mixed
borders, but their arrangement indicates
the taste of an artist. And a vast meadow,
stretching out in front of a fairy-tale
cottage, enshrines an impeccably
manicured croquet lawn with grass as soft
and deep as a Wilton carpet. To cross the
river, you go over a Victorian teak bridge.
On the other side, a wall's alignment of
stones draws attention, making you
wonder: is it some prehistoric construction like those strewn over the moor
around the property or is it a natural
heap of rocks? This same game of illusions
persists inside the house.

In the hall, paneled in light oak, a
Siamese cat sleeps in front of the fireplace
where a fire burns continuously. In one
corner, a grandfather clock ticks out the
hours—which can only be pleasant, given
the hotel's plush, pampered atmosphere
that encourages *dolce far niente* and a

Photo on pages 214 and 215:
*A cyclopean wall runs through the underwood.
A masterpiece of nature or the work of man?*

"*Devant moi, la campagne est d'un vert
que je peux dire multicolore.*"
Jules Renard

Dining tête-à-tête to appreciate the inventive cuisine of Chef Shaun Hill.

There is nothing like a whiskey porridge and a solid breakfast before a walk in the moors.

No bothersome curtain gets in the way of the soothing view of the garden.

vacation from worry. In the large drawing room, the walls are wainscoted with small panels ornamented with Louis XV-style appliqués. Light floods into the room from three immense bow windows whose splayings shelter window seats and cushions covered in floral chintz. An armada of leather easy chairs and sofas, as deep as tombs, invite reading or dreaming on rainy days. At the center of the drawing room, a large octagonal mahogany table offers a selection of various magazines. And a desk and stationery are provided for any guest who wishes to write.

Gidleigh Park offers the same discreet luxury and the same attention to details in its dozen rooms and two suites. All display a typically British sense of intimacy and comfort. Fruit baskets and bouquets of fresh flowers decorate the tables. In the bathrooms, towels warming on special radiators and thick terry cloth bathrobes await as you step out of the shower or tub. The bathrooms, which pair the cold beauty of marble with the warmth of lacquered wood, are equipped with sumptuous taps dating from the beginning of the century. With their canopies, curtains, valances, and quilts, the beds unfurl almost as much fabric as a Navy ship once hoisted in full sail. The rooms are furnished with a couch, antique commodes, pedestals, and upholstered armchairs. What a pleasure it is to be surrounded by them on blustery days. When the wind howls in the nearby forest, you can sit, cozy and snug, rereading cases cracked by Sherlock Holmes or Hercule Poirot, or a suspense novel by Ruth Rendell before sinking into sleep.

A main staircase links the rooms to

The charm of a wood fire in the large drawing room.

A row of boots, raincoats, and umbrellas in the vestibule; the prudent panoply for a weekend in Devon.

*A flowered room's space and brightness invites
a longer stay* (right).

*The hall at Gidleigh Park exudes warm British
hospitality* (below).

the public quarters below. At the bottom of the steps, a copper gong evokes the past splendors of the British Empire. The gong is no longer solemnly struck to announce the dinner hour, but wearing a jacket and tie to the dining room is still appreciated. At night, the bar is an agreeable stop before dinner. Here guests can sip a glass of wine, an old Port, or a whiskey while watching the night slowly encroach on the park.

Niches, set into the dining room's light-yellow walls, display a collection of crystal carafes and English porcelains. The tables are covered with carefully starched tablecloths. Nature, which surrounds Gidleigh Park, also makes its presence felt in the menu ingredients. Inventive and light, the dishes are prepared with herbs and vegetables from the garden by Chef Shaun Hill, one of the few Englishmen to have ever been elected to the French culinary academy.

This blend of tradition and innovation, of the natural and the sophisticated, could well be the distinguishing mark of Gidleigh Park, deservedly praised by the severe Egon Ronay guide as the quintessential "country house hotel."

*The large oak staircase is illuminated by light co
through a spectacular lattice-work bow win
An exuberant, freshly picked bouque
on the mahogany t*

CHEWTON GLEN

~

The paradox of a sophisticated palace hotel
set in the landscape of Tess of the D'Ubervilles

The nineteenth-century French humorist Alphonse Allais recommended setting up cities in the country. The proprietors of Chewton Glen, Bridget and Martin Skan, have followed his advice—on a more modest scale. They have created a palace—a true haven of civilization and comfort in the middle of fields. Chewton Glen is located in the New Forest, an area in the southwest of England. At one time, William the Conqueror and the Normans depopulated this region in order to turn it into a royal hunting preserve. Since then, despite the scourges of industrialization and urbanization, the New Forest has remained a rural area. Stags continue to throng the woods, herds of ponies roam freely in the countryside, and trout and salmon still proliferate in the rivers.

The privileged enclave of Chewton Glen, comprising forty hectares of woods, meadows, lawns, and admirably tended gardens, stretches out between the ancient forests of Hampshire and the sea, almost directly opposite the Isle of Wight. The manor dates back to the beginning of the eighteenth century when the English countryside was dotted with pleasant mansions in the Palladian style. Built on this neoclassical model, Chewton Glen later yielded to the nineteenth-century rage for pastiche and eclecticism. In the 1830s the main façade was adorned with semicircular bow windows and a large veranda in the style made fashionable by the London architect John Nash. Later, at the height of the Victorian era, the façade was bricked in the Queen Anne style.

Chewton Glen had its hour of glory during the 1840s when the writer Frederick Marryat stayed here. Somewhat forgotten today, Marryat had a distinguished career as a captain in the British Navy, waging war in Asia and hunting smugglers on the English Channel. Captain Marryat liked to rest from his toils at sea at his brother's home, Chewton Glen. At the manor, Marryat wrote maritime adventure novels that enjoyed a certain success. During his stays in the country, he also gathered stories and details about the New Forest and its denizens, who were passionately

The comfort of a wood fire in the small drawing room. Bouquets of dried flowers are reflected in the neoclassical pier glass.

Under the knowing gaze of a cricket player, the outfit of an accomplished sportsman: fishing, riding, tennis and golf gear, and of course, the croquet set.

227

*On the landing, a still life with soup tureen.
Its contents are less restorative than perfumed:
a potpourri of dried flowers (right).*

*The intimacy of Chewton Glen's bar. The walls
are covered by a striped old-rose and taupe
fabric, setting off the blue sofas and armchairs.
The curved niches protect the books' antique
bindings (below).*

devoted to one particular sport: smuggling. On the shore nearby, they unloaded bales of tobacco, tea, and silk, and barrels of wine and alcohol; at night they set out for the interior with their contraband. Inspired by this local "exploit," Marryat wrote *The Children of the New Forest*, his most famous novel, in 1847. Chewton Glen's bar was named after this notable guest—followed by many others, some even more notable. The rooms also honor his memory by bearing the names of characters in his books, and a showcase in the hall exhibits a number of souvenirs of this sea dog turned writer.

The manor had long since stopped being the Marryat family residence when the Skans purchased Chewton Glen in 1966. Recalls Bridget with an amused smile, "There were only eight rooms all in all, and only one had a bathroom!" Seeing Chewton Glen today, we can easily gauge the amount of work accomplished since renovations were begun, all with a zeal and a concern for perfection that clearly never wavered. Martin Skan conceived and executed the hotel's modernization plan, as well as its practical improvements. His success has been recognized and honored by an impressive list of awards: Chewton Glen belongs to the prestigious Relais et Châteaux chain, the Leading Hotels in the World, and is

Photos on pages 222, 223, 224 and 225:

Page 222: *English still life in the hall. Two retrievers flank a free spirit of the New Forest, painted in 1883. Chewton Glen offers the choice of sport or leisure: golf clubs or plaid blanket?*

Page 223: *The original manor, at the center, with its recent enlargements. The wing on the right contains rooms; the one on the left, a Palladian temple devoted to the cult of Poseidon encloses a beautiful indoor swimming pool.*

Pages 224 and 225: *As in a Merchant-Ivory film, the deliciously old-fashioned charm of a croquet game played in front of one of Chewton Glen's façades.*

*The Victorian bow accentuates a "witch" mirror that reflects
the main hall's white and straw-yellow colors. In the center,
a lion-clawed Regency table holds the guest register.*

the only English hotel outside of London that has been decorated with the Five Gold Crown Award by the British Tourist Office. The hotel has also earned the Michelin Guide's rarely bestowed designation of five "red houses," signifying excellence.

Bridget Skan decorated Chewton Glen's interior. Under her guidance, each room has been arranged and decorated differently, but all were done in such a manner as to offer guests every possible comfort while still making them feel at home—not an easy task when you take into account the size of the hotel, the number of rooms (sixty-two, including thirteen suites), and the large staff: one hundred forty people. "Each room should, in my opinion, have a certain number of antiques: a desk, a commode, and antique chairs," specifies Bridget. This period furniture, like the hotel's paintings, engravings, objets d'art, and fine porcelains, was scoured from antiques dealers in every country. The furniture is enhanced by the most beautiful English fabrics, elegantly arranged by a London draper and lavished as generously on the rooms as on the salons. Bouquets of fresh flowers and dried ones, providing perfect harmony with the colors in the rooms, enliven pedestals and consoles. This same

scrupulous attention to the authenticity and quality of every finishing led Martin to obtain one million bricks and antique tiles to enlarge Chewton Glen using original materials. Likewise, when the Skans decided to build an indoor pool, they respected the architecture of the site by housing the pool inside a Palladian temple. The structure is so well integrated with the manor that intrigued guests always ask about the building's original purpose.

Recently, Chewton Glen added a resort spa, offering a mere thirty or so possible beauty and health treatments. This addition has allowed the hotel to diversify and rejuvenate its usual clientele of businessmen. Guests are free to pursue whatever activities they please, all provided with an inimitable British sense of comfort and intimacy. The management has set a golden rule for itself: "The hotel should try to offer whatever a guest desires." Abiding by it has made Chewton Glen one of the most civilized places on either side of the English Channel or the Atlantic.

Sherlock Holmes would have approved this dictum. And fans of the phlegmatic detective have yet another reason to visit Chewton Glen. His creator, Sir Arthur Conan Doyle, rests not far from here at the church of Minstead.

View from the baluster terrace onto the Florentine-style swimming pool bordered with cypresses and yew trees. The hydrangeas add a more English touch to the scene. . . .

A room under the hotel's mansard roof. The draper's art is triumphantly displayed in everything from the curtains and bedspreads to the cushions and table skirts.

The golf course at the bottom of the terrace; one of the many sports activities available at Chewton Glen.

Blakes

~

A cosmopolitan aesthete creates a jewel-box hotel in London

It could be the palace of a maharaja, the whim of an Oriental sultan, the "folly" of a Russian prince at the time of the czars, or the townhouse of such refined decadents as Joris-Karl Huysmans' Des Esseintes or Walter Pater's Charles de Rosenmold. Baudelaire would have appreciated this symphony of black, purple, and gold, evoking the fiery union of Eros and Thanatos, and it could well have inspired Rimbaud's famous sonnet "Voyelles." "There is only one Blakes," says the celebrated designer Anouska Hempel. The hotel's mistress and muse states this without excessive modesty but with

just cause. Blakes is her masterpiece. A paragon of originality and the quintessence of luxury and refinement, the hotel is the fruit of her travels around the world, reflecting her finds, her elective affinities, her reminiscences, her wanderings among the antiques dealers of every country—in short, the sum of a life dedicated to the pleasure of others.

Blakes is in Roland Gardens in the elegant London district of South Kensington, not far from Chelsea. The hotel's dark green—almost black—façade stands out clearly against the row of redbrick apartment buildings, lined up as if on parade, of Roland Gardens.

The bow elegantly tied around the candlestick makes all the difference (opposite).

Three views of the hotel's inner court. A monochrome of greens: dark green for the brick wall, soft green for the potted box trees, bright green for the laurels pruned into ball shapes, jade green for the Asian vases.

Photos on pages 232 and 233:

Page 232: *Blakes foyer reflected in the "witch" mirror. Right away the hotel's tone is set: black as the dominant color, sophistication, and a cultivation of the unique.*

Page 233: *The hotel's dark green façade stands out among the row of conventional redbrick apartment buildings in Roland Gardens (top). Glimpse into a room. Each detail has the stamp of originality (bottom).*

The sensation of being in another world is confirmed as soon as you enter Blakes. Anouska Hempel obviously does not share her countrymen's atavistic predilection for floral prints, striped and trelliswork wallpapers, or for the mix of colors and patterns that were rife during the Victorian era and that so aroused Oscar Wilde's criticism during his American lectures on house decoration. But the decor at Blakes makes it just as clear that Anouska Hempel does not prize the restraint of the modern style or the spare look of the arts and crafts movement. Judging by the decoration and the furnishings in her hotel, Hempel is among the category of people who renowned Italian critic Mario Praz saved from damnation. In his *Illustrated History of Furnishing*, Praz wrote, "I confess that it is extremely difficult for me to understand the soul of men who do not care for their possessions or their houses. . . . The man who has no interest in his house and who is not moved by the harmony of handsome furnishings is for me, as for Shakespeare, the man who 'hath no music in himself . . . is fit for treasons, stratagems, and spoils; the motions of his spirit are dull as night, and his affections dark as Erebus.'" Every detail at Blakes and every decorative element reveals a passionate concern for aesthetics

and for what Henry James called "the mysteries of ministration to rare pieces."

As soon as you enter the foyer, Blakes evokes Baudelaire's "invitation to the voyage," enticing you to stroll through eras and continents. Above the staircase leading to the restaurant, an immense teak parasol with a wide top of unbleached linen extends its shade as if the tropical sun had somehow wandered into this London enclave. Bamboo couches and armchairs introduce an Oriental note, while a group of cabin trunks and old canteens suggest the return from a jungle expedition or the preparations for boarding an ocean liner. And adding to the foyer's exotic atmosphere, a green-and-yellow parrot in a gilded cage squawks, every once in a while, a cry of astonishment. . . .

A handsome inner court is located at the back of the hotel. Once as gray as a rainy day in London, the court has been transformed as if by the touch of a magic wand. A monochrome of green shades blossoms around a teak table and armchairs, reflected in a huge mirror resting against a wall: dark green for the bricks, jade green for the Chinese vases, glossy green for the topiary box trees. More of these potted bushes adorn the

This wall of leather-bound books, turning amber with time, partly conceals a bar and a garderobe.

A prologue to feeling you are in another world: like an explorer's room, the foyer at Blakes has Chinese armchairs, cabin trunks, a huge tropical parasol, and a birdcage where a parrot ruffles its feathers (opposite, top).

White also has a place at Blakes. The milky white and the bluish white in this room evoke eighteenth-century Swedish interiors (opposite, bottom).

A theatrically raised curtain in black, red, and gold. Each room is characterized by a different, but always sumptuous bed (right).

The bathrooms harmonize with the rooms. In this bathroom, the walls imitate tortoiseshell, and the sabot-shaped bathtub could well have welcomed the legendary Prince of Wales (below).

windowsills on the first floor, as if to brighten the Italian-style grilles that protect the windows.

In the basement, the hotel's restaurant and its small adjoining salon give a nod to the Orient, but to a purified Orient, all in geometric lines. A splendid screen from Coromandel unfolds against the walls of the small salon. On a coffee table, art books are stacked in thick, impressive layers like geological strata. Surrounding the table, sofas piled high with mountains of cushions represent the room's sole concession to the Victorian taste for stuffing and padding. The restaurant itself is decorated with ancient ethnic costumes of Asian and Latin-American origin, splashing the walls with their bright colors.

Two staircases lead to the rooms. One is painted a gray-taupe color, while the other is sponge painted and given a yellow-ocher patina. Discreet fragrances waft from porcelain and metal bowls filled with potpourris or dried lavender, set on window ledges and consoles. The room decor at Blakes is dramatic, and your astonishment will begin as soon as you glimpse one of the fifty rooms and suites in the hotel. Each is different, but all reflect Anouska Hempel's unique style. A blend of opulence, sophistication, provocation, and theatricality, her sense of style

A luxurious bed inviting poetic dreams.

nevertheless embraces the taste for comfort so dear to the British. What is most striking at first is the warm, almost too rich atmosphere created by the dominant colors—black, purple, ocher, gold—and by the materials and the painterly effects used. Silk cascades in heavy spirals from the testers and curtain pelmets over the canopy beds. The walls are covered with rare and precious trompe l'oeil such as tortoiseshell or the look of leather binding. The ceilings unveil a rich gamut of clouded and wiped decorating effects. The floors are either carpeted with sisal laid against the nap or imitation marble polychrome marquetry. In these confined and sumptuous jewel-box rooms, like Raphael's loggias or Madame de Pompadour's small private apartments at Versailles, everything radiates in the words of the poet Baudelaire, "luxe, calme et volupté."

Blakes pays particular homage to the bed. By itself, the hotel could fill an anthology dedicated to this furniture that prosaic spirits with no imagination treat only as a simple accessory in which to sleep. At Blakes, however, beds are enthroned in the middle of the rooms like monarchs in their audience chambers. Canopy beds, Polish-style beds, duchess beds, boat beds, gondola beds, tomb beds, Roman beds, roller beds, Empire beds, Biedermeier beds, Gustavian beds, Napoleon III beds, Victorian beds, Belle Epoque beds—you would be hard put to

Heavy black-and-gold silk curtains for the hotel's canopy beds. The beds are lavished with a wealth of cushions and are perched up high in the style of the seventeenth and eighteenth centuries.

themes, sometimes so numerous that they cover an entire wall.

Contrary to the decorating arrangements customarily found in England, the placement of the furniture and of the frames and mirrors reveals a very classical taste for symmetry. This unprecedented marriage of baroque and classicism, exuberance and restraint, constitutes the hotel's distinctive stamp. Thus, rooms featuring richly contrasted decors with dark tonalities are found next to rooms devoted to light colors such as gray or white—but these are not bland colors: the gray vibrates with infinite nuances, while the white is lit up by blue as in eighteenth-century Swedish interiors.

The most sober rooms appear to have an echo of the Adam brothers who created the taste for bright, fresh rooms decorated without ostentation during the Age of Enlightenment. Elsewhere, the dominant hues derive from a desired harmony with a painting or reflect a very modern bias for monochrome. In all the rooms, indirect, dimmer, and auxiliary lights diffuse a muted glow that accentuates contrasts in the decor in the style of such masters of chiaroscuro as the seventeenth-century French painter Georges de la Tour. The bathrooms show the same

find a single type of bed that has escaped Anouska Hempel's passion for collecting. Majestic as temples, high as ships, deep as catafalques, intimate as alcoves, and decorated as shrines, the beds at Blakes seem to invite you to do everything, except perhaps sleep. We can easily imagine the Marquise de Rambouillet holding a salon here with the précieuses of the "blue room," Madame Récamier posing for posterity, Victor Hugo improvising a hymn to the "divine creaking of trestle beds," the Prince of Wales forgetting his sacrosanct Puritan principles, and Marcel Proust spending feverish nights, with all the curtains drawn, finishing *Remembrance of Things Past*. The variety of beds offered is so great that we would like to try all of them one after another. But no doubt some enthusiast will turn up to accept this challenge. . . . Although the beds are the rooms' pièces de résistance, they are complimented by commodes, tables, and antique libraries in either identical or harmonious styles. The rooms also display paintings or collections of engravings on particular

Page 243:
Atop a canopy bed, a peaceful lion watches over the guests' sleep.

An extraordinary Napoleon III-style cabinet inlaid with flower and bird motifs. The cabinet is framed on both sides by a series of engravings on the theme of bed decorating.

studied elegance and refinement in their assortment of colors and choice of materials. Some have black lacquer or black marble with gleaming antique copper taps, or inversely, ocher marble and light-yellow tortoiseshell. As in the rooms, the walls in the bathrooms are hung with engravings, often climbing so high they practically touch the ceiling.

This celebration of decor and style is accompanied by all the most sophisticated amenities. However, Blakes would not have inspired the ironic judgment of a nineteenth-century traveler from Vienna who liked to go against the grain of conventional ideas. The lady exclaimed, "Comfort, comfort, the English always have this word on their lips, and it's precisely in England that I have found the least amount of comfort. Nowhere have I suffered so much from the cold, even inside. The fire may warm up the person who is sitting right beside the fireplace and who has nothing else to do but keep warm—but not the person who is a little further away and who is busy writing or sewing. What wonderful comfort in a country where you have to fight the cold six or seven months of the year!"

But Blakes does offer every comfort. Now we understand: if England is still an island, Blakes remains an island in the heart of London. An oasis of civilization that fulfills Cocteau's famous injunction: "Astonish me!" The hotel is an inexhaustible source of surprises: a rare and ideal place to forget how much of life is humdrum, to enjoy a diversion from the fogs of London, to yield to a fatal attraction, to offer yourself an interlude of the "inimitable life," or to end your days, like Oscar Wilde, living above your means.

Primarily in a patina gray, this room is adorned with a rare antique bed (top).

An astounding Napoleon III bed paired with the cabinet opposite. Elegant and delicate night tables on both sides of the bed hold up lamps mounted on bases formed from antique ankle boots (right).

THE PELHAM

~

*The love of tradition blended
with a taste for the unique*

Unlike bland, anonymous hotel halls, the entrance to the Pelham manifests the hotel's sense of hospitality by its wealth of colors and plush upholstery (opposite).

A staircase in all its Victorian majesty (below, left).

This telephone dial seems to remind us that life is an obstacle course (below, right).

Nestled between Chelsea and Hyde Park, South Kensington is comparable to no other neighborhood in London. Harboring bastions of respectability such as Christie's and the Victoria and Albert Museum, South Kensington is characterized by a lively and cosmopolitan atmosphere. Cafés with glass awnings set their tables out on the sidewalk, and children from the Lycée Français walk down the street chattering in French. Renowned art galleries stand next to small antique shops, select restaurants rub shoulders with Polish bars that serve borscht and meatballs, and the bright colors of street-corner florists add to the elegance of the leafy gardens on Thames Square. South Kensington displays its own distinctive style—leave the anonymous opulence of Knightsbridge and Mayfair to those who like it; the traveler who stays at the Pelham Hotel on Cromwell Place is a person of taste who appreciates tradition while venturing to be different.

Like an English gentleman who casually sports brightly colored suspenders under his tweed suit or manifests a preference for silk embroidered pajamas, the Pelham Hotel is proud of its individuality but does not proclaim it. The hotel's brilliantly white portico

Photos on pages 246 and 247:

Page 246: *Cromwell Place reflected in the hotel's sparkling copper plaque; its anachronistic cavalier makes sport of the street's traffic jams.*

Page 247: *Nature stakes a claim even in the heart of London* (top).
A well-advised gentleman never leaves without his umbrella or the wherewithal to light his cigar (bottom).

façade is as impressive as any other in the heart of South Kensington, but nothing behind the Pelham's polished door is old-fashioned. The decor immediately sets the tone: every detail reflects good old English tradition, not the soulless replica of some English manor. The hall's flirtatious three-seat sofa is upholstered in a checked red-and-navy blue fabric, not in a peaked-looking velvet. The portrait of great-grandaunt Eliza, appearing straitlaced but oddly red-faced above the liquor tray, is wreathed with dried lavender. And the hotel's swagger and swathed curtains are nothing but flamboyant. Everywhere there are fresh flowers—in great armfuls that look as if they came straight from the fields, or in bouquets of morning glories or campanulas set in antique glass bottles.

These little touches make you feel immediately at home and invite you to discover the hotel. What better place to start than by drinking tea in the drawing room after a long day hunting for some treasure in the city's auction houses and galleries? The eighteenth-century drawing room is paneled in pine. Above the fireplace hangs the portrait of a gentleman in wig and jabot whose stern face seems to rejuvenate with the warmth of the crackling fire. Later, after tea, where better to satisfy your hunger than in Pelham's excellent dining room? The walls are lined with midnight blue engravings bearing gold stars representing the hotel's namesake: the steeplechase

The drawing room evokes the refined ambience of Jane Austen's novels. Its decor includes light-yellow pine paneling, wing chairs, a chandelier with crystal pendants, and a carved chimneypiece crowned by the portrait of a bewigged gentleman.

In her floral frame, a Victorian lady watches over the mahogany-paneled smoking room (below, left).

rider Pelham Suite dashing forward on a horse.

Perhaps your thirst for discovery will be slaked when you enter your room. From the most sumptuous suites on the first floor, with their high rococo ceilings and their chandeliers, to the comfortable rooms niched in the eaves, every room is magnificently decorated.

If a man's house reveals his character, the hotels where he chooses to stay unveil his sense of style. The Pelham Hotel's delicate blend of originality and classic English quality will appeal to lovers of tradition with a taste for the distinctive.

"Accalmie et tiédeur humide,
et odeur de miel du tabac ;
La dorure de ce livre
Devient plus claire à chaque instant :
un essai de soleil sans doute."
Valery Larbaud

One of the suites on the first floor; the elegant decor awakes a desire to settle into the hotel permanently, as Coco Chanel once did at the Ritz.

Another suite at the Pelham Hotel. The sumptuous canopy bed is not the least of the room's ornaments. All the rooms are distinguished by their own particular decor, but all feature high-quality antique furniture, paintings or engravings, bouquets of fresh flowers and other signs of civilization.

CHÂTEAU DE BAGNOLS

- *Activities: tennis, horseback riding, hot-air ballooning, golf course nearby, touring Beaujolais wine region.*
- *45 min. from Lyons Satolas airport.*
- *69620 Bagnols, France.*
- *Tel.: 74.71.40.00*
- *Fax: 74.71.40.49*

HÔTEL DE ROSIER

- *Activities: swimming pool, sauna, visiting Antwerp.*
- *25 min. from Antwerp airport.*
- *Rue Rosier, 21-23 B-2000, Antwerp, Belgium.*
- *Tel.: (32-3) 225.01.40*
- *Fax: (32-3) 231.41.11*

CHÂTEAU DE PRUNOY

- *Restaurant in the hotel.*
- *Activities: resort spa, swimming pool, tennis, cycling, boat excursions on the property's ponds.*
- *89120 Charny, France.*
- *Tel.: 86.63.66.91*
- *Fax: 86.63.77.79*

CASA DE CARMONA

- *Restaurant in the hotel.*
- *Activities: swimming pool, walking tours of the area.*
- *10 min. from Seville airport.*
- *Plaza de Lasso, Carmona, Seville, Spain.*
- *Tel.: (95) 414.33.00*
- *Fax: (95) 414.37.52*

HÔTEL DE LA MIRANDE

- *Restaurant in the hotel.*
- *Activities: private garden, sauna, jacuzzi, theater festival.*
- *20 min. from Avignon airport.*
- *Place de la Mirande, 84000 Avignon, France.*
- *Tel.: 90.85.93.93*
- *Fax: 90.86.26.85*

HACIENDA BENAZUZA

- *3 restaurants in the hotel.*
- *Activities: swimming pool, tennis, jacuzzi, putting green at the hotel. Golf, hunting, and horseback riding nearby.*
- *Virgen de las nieves S/N, 41800 Sanlúcar la Mayor, Seville, Spain.*
- *Tel.: (95) 5703344 • Fax: (95) 5703410*

CHÂTEAU DE REMAISNIL

- *Restaurant: table d'hôte.*
- *Activities: billiards, horseback riding, hunting.*
- *1 hr. 30 min. from Roissy-Charles-de-Gaulle airport in Paris.*
- *80600 Doullens (Picardy), France.*
- *Tel.: 22.77.07.47*
- *Fax: 22.32.43.27*

DROMOLAND CASTLE

- *Restaurant in the hotel.*
- *Activities: golf course in a 400-acre park, tennis, hunting, fishing, horseback riding, billiards, Ping-Pong.*
- *20 min. from Shannon airport.*
- *Newmarket-on-Fergus, County Clare, Ireland.*
- *Tel.: (061) 36.81.44 • Fax: (061) 36.33.55*

GRAND HÔTEL NORD PINUS

- *Restaurant in the hotel.*
- *Activities: Photo exhibits, corridas, tours of the surrounding Camargue. • 1 hr. 30 min. from the international airport of Marseilles Marignane and 25 min. from airport in Nîmes.*
- *Place du Forum, 13200 Arles-en-Provence, France.*
- *Tel.: 90.93.44.44 • Fax: 90.93.34.00*

HÔTEL PALACIO DE SETEAIS

- *Restaurant in the hotel.*
- *Activities: swimming pool, tennis, horseback riding. Near the sea and Grand Prix Formula 1 racetrack at Estoril.*
- *27 km. from Lisbon airport.*
- *Rua Barbosa Do Bocage N-8, 2710 Sintra, Portugal.*
- *Tel.: (01) 92.33.200 • Fax: (01) 92.34.277*

LLANGOED HALL

- *Restaurant in the hotel.*
- *Activities: fishing, hunting, tennis, billiards, croquet, golf, and nearby trail-riding tours.*
- *1 hr. 15 min. from Cardiff airport.*
- *Llyswen Brecon Powys, Wales, LD30YP.*
- *Tel.: (0874) 75.45.25*
- *Fax: (0874) 75.45.45*

TORRE DI BELLOSGUARDO

- *Restaurant by the swimming pool during the summer.*
- *Activities: swimming pool, touring Florence and Tuscany.*
- *15 min. from Peretola airport in Florence, 1 hr. from Pisa airport.*
- *Via Roti Michelozzi, 2, Florence, Italy.*
- *Tel.: (055) 2298145 • Fax: (055) 229008*

SCHLOSSHOTEL KRONBERG

- *Restaurant in the hotel.*
- *Activities: 18-hole golf course, rose garden.*
- *30 min. from Frankfurt airport.*
- *Hainstrasse 25, D-6242, Kronberg im Taunus, Germany.*
- *Tel.: (061.73) 70101*
- *Fax: (061.73) 701267*

GIDLEIGH PARK

- *Restaurant in the hotel.*
- *Activities: fishing, hunting, croquet, walking trails in the property's 20-hectare park and in adjacent Dartmoor National Park.*
- *Chagford, Devon, TQ 138 HH, England.*
- *Tel.: (0647) 43.23.67*
- *Fax: (0647) 43.25.74*

HÔTEL PALUMBO

- *Restaurant in the hotel.*
- *Activities: solarium, swimming pool, tennis nearby, tour of the Amalfi coastline. Production of estate wine.*
- *Via San Giovanni del Toro, 28 84010 Ravello, Italy.*
- *Tel.: (089) 857244*
- *Fax: (089) 858133*

CHEWTON GLEN

- *Restaurant in the hotel.*
- *Activities: resort spa, indoor and outdoor swimming pools, Turkish baths, saunas, croquet, golf, two indoor tennis courts.*
- *Christchurch Road, New Milton, Hampshire, BH25 6QS, England.*
- *Tel.: (0425) 275341 • Fax: (0425) 27 23 10*
- *Toll free from USA: 1 800 344 5087*

GRAND HÔTEL EXCELSIOR VITTORIA

- *Restaurant in the hotel*
- *Activities: swimming pool, fishing and excursions at sea, touring the Amalfi coastline. • 50 km. from Naples airport.*
- *Piazza T. Tasso, 34 Sorrento, Naples, Italy.*
- *Tel.: (081) 8071044 • Fax: (081) 8771206*

BLAKES HOTEL

- *Restaurant in the hotel.*
- *Activities: 5 min. from the center of London.*
- *45 min. from Heathrow International airport.*
- *33 Roland Gardens, London SW 7, England.*
- *Tel.: (071) 370 67 01 • Fax: (071) 373 04 42*

CERTOSA DI MAGGIANO

- *Restaurant in the hotel.*
- *Activities: tennis, swimming pool, touring Siena, horseback riding, visiting the wine cellars of Chianti and Brunello.*
- *60 km. from Peretola airport in Florence.*
- *Strada di Certosa, 82, 53100 Siena, Italy.*
- *Tel.: (0577) 28.81.80*
- *Fax: (0577) 28.81.89*

THE PELHAM HOTEL

- *Restaurant in the hotel.*
- *Activities: touring London.*
- *15 Cromwell Place, London SW7 2LA, England.*
- *Tel.: (071) 5898288*
- *Fax: (071) 5848444*
- *Toll free from USA: 1 800 553 6671*

Nicholas Démians d'Archimbaud would like to thank:
All the hotel owners who agreed to lodge us for free and without whose contributions this work could not have come true.
Daniel Czap and Jean-Louis Bloch-Lainé for their enlightened instructions.
Claudia Bensi for her radiant presence and Salvatore Pagano for several fits of uncontrollable laughter.
Anne-Rita Crestani, Sandrine Ely, and many others for their contribution to this book and for their support.
Serge Maestracci and Frédéric Versluys for their valuable help during the early stages of this book.

Texts:
SÉVERINE JOUVE: *Château de Prunoy, Château de Bagnols, La Mirande, Grand Hôtel Nord Pinus, Torre di Bellosguardo, Certosa di Maggiano, Excelsior Vittoria, Palumbo.*
THIERRY WOLTON: *Casa de Carmona, Palacio de Seteais, Hacienda Benazuza, Dromoland Castle, Hôtel De Rosier, Schlosshotel Kronberg, Château de Remaisnil.*
BRUNO DE CESSOLE: *Gidleigh Park Hotel, Chewton Glen, Llangoed Hall, Blakes, Pelham.*